The Flight to Objectivity

SUNY Series in Philosophy
Robert C. Neville, Editor

The Flight to Objectivity

Essays on Cartesianism and Culture

Susan Bordo

STATE UNIVERSITY OF NEW YORK PRESS

Published by
State University of New York Press, Albany

© 1987   State University of New York

For information, address State University of New York Press,
State University Plaza, Albany, N.Y., 12246

Library of Congress Cataloging-in-Publication Data

Bordo, Susan, 1947-
  The flight to objectivity.

  (SUNY series in philosophy)
  Bibliography: p. 133
  Includes index.
  1. Descartes, René, 1596-1650. Meditationes de prima
philosophia. 2. First philosophy. I. Title. II. Series.
B1854.B67   1987   194   87-10066
ISBN 0-88706-410-8
ISBN 0-887-6-411-6 (pbk.)

10 9 8 7 6 5 4 3 2 1

*This book is dedicated to my father, Julius Alexander Klein,
and in remembrance of my mother, Regina Lillian Klein*

Contents

Acknowledgements

This study was first conceived more than six years ago, out of my growing sense that a variety of intellectual currents, in philosophy, cultural history, and feminism, were converging around issues concerning the birth of modern science. Since then, the central ideas of the study have been refracted through the perspectives of many friends, colleagues, and students. All the intellectual communities that I have worked within have influenced my thinking and thus shaped this work: the philosophy department of the State University of New York at Stony Brook, the Federated Learning Communities of SUNY/Stony Brook, the philosophy department of Le Moyne College, and the community of feminist scholars, which extends across disciplines and departments.

When the ideas of this study were still inchoate, the empathic insights and philosophical imaginations of Patrick Hill, C. Lee Miller, and Mario Moussa provided the encouragement without which the study probably would not have been continued. C. Lee Miller read and provided extensive, detailed, and enormously helpful comments on the first draft. Patrick Hill, Janice McLane, Mario Moussa, Edward Casey, Robert Neville, and Rose Zimbardo also provided invaluable criticism and support at this stage.

Between the first and second drafts, the central "argument" of the study was distilled into an article, "The Cartesian Masculinization of Thought," which was published in Signs (Volume 11, Number 3). Those who helped me prepare and revise that article — Mario Moussa, Carolyn Merchant, Barbara Gelpi, and Mary Wyer — also helped me to crystallize the ideas of the larger study. In Spring 1985, I participated, as a Visiting Scholar, in the "Feminist Reconstructions of Self and Society" seminar at Douglass College, Rutgers University; our stimulating weekly meetings, and the encouragement and insight of Alison Jaggar in particular, informed and motivated me in writing the second draft. That draft was carefully read by Mario Moussa, who helped me to discern certain key themes that had not been adequately brought out, and who provided many useful stylistic and philosophical suggestions. I am grateful for his support and advice at all stages of this project.

The final draft was painstakingly read by Lynne Arnault, whose keen eye for obscurity made this a clearer and more readable work. Her philosophical understanding and editorial acumen contributed greatly to establishing continuity and coherence within the study's somewhat unorthodox structure.

Whatever lack of coherence or clarity may remain is, of course, solely my own responsibility. The typing of the manuscript was provided for by two faculty research grants from Le Moyne College.

Finally, Edward Lee has been a constant source of support, tirelessly willing to discuss ideas at all stages and at any time, providing much-needed encouragement when my spirit flagged, and contributing his own penetrating insights into contemporary culture and intellectual history.

Abbreviations

HR *The Philosophical Works of Descartes*, edited and translated by Elizabeth Haldane and G.R.T. Ross, Cambridge, Cambridge University Press, 1911; reprinted 1969, 2 volumes.

PL *Descartes: Philosophical Letters*, translated and edited by Anthony Kenny, Oxford, Clarendon Press, 1970.

B *Descartes' Conversation with Burman*, translated with introduction and commentary by John Cottingham, Oxford, Clarendon Press, 1976.

Introduction

On November 10, 1619, Descartes had a series of dreams — bizarre, richly image-laden sequences manifestly full of anxiety and dread. He interpreted these dreams — which most readers would surely regard as nightmares — as revealing to him that mathematics is the key to understanding the universe.[1] Descartes's resolute and disconcertingly positive interpretation has become a standard textbook anecdote, a symbol of the seventeenth-century rationalist project. That project, in the official story told in most philosophy and history texts, describes seventeenth-century culture as Descartes described in his dreams: in terms of intellectual beginnings and fresh confidence, and a new belief in the ability of science — armed with the discourses of mathematics and the "new philosophy" — to decipher the language of nature.

Such a "reading" of Descartes and the culture within which he wrote was continuous with and appropriate to what was, until fairly recently, widespread confidence in modern science and faith in its projects. Now that that faith has been undermined, the nightmare quality of Descartes's dream is reasserting itself. Not very long ago, the present had been experienced in terms of continuity (sometimes uneasy, but intimate, implicit) with the objectivist, mechanist presuppositions of modern science. Today, we look back on

1

the Cartesian promise of absolute epistemic objectivity and ultimate foundations for knowledge from an ever more critical distance, as ideals which have
run their course. The limitations of science and the interested, even
ideological nature of all human pursuits now seem unavoidable recognitions.
Regularly, we learn from the media of the carcinogenic properties of
substances once thought to be benign or even life-saving. Ecological and
industrial disasters prove to be the result of measures initially believed to
serve human progress. Conventional assumptions and definitions of "life"
and "personhood" are challenged by technological advances that overstep
each other with such rapidity that we cannot avoid questioning the very
possibility of a conceptual grasp of such notions. Long-standing traditions in
scientific and ethical rationality have been exposed as harboring class, racial,
and sexual biases. Surrounded by "isms" and barraged by openly competing
frameworks of explanation, students exhibit an anxiety psychologically akin
to the contemporary philosophical insecurity described so well by Richard
Rorty: Can we ever know anything at all, they wonder, if all "knowledge"
is a matter of human construction and social convention?

The mood of intellectual histories of modernity is ominous, funereal:
concerning the Cartesian-Newtonian world view, writers speak of a "turning
point," "an outdated world view," "a crisis in perception," (Capra) "an inherent instability" that "has destroyed the continuity of human experience and
the integrity of the human psyche [and] very nearly wrecked the planet as
well" (Berman, 23). But even if the dominant mood were not that of crisis
and critique, a decisive rupture would still be signalled by the fact that we
are now grasping "modernity," "the scientific paradigm," "the Cartesian
model," as discrete, contained, historical entities about which coherent "clos-
ing" narratives can be told. In many different academic arenas, from history
of science to literary theory, we find fewer and fewer open adherents to the
Cartesian dream; more and more have begun to critically objectify it: to
historicize it, to psychoanalyze it, to deconstruct it.

The pivotal philosophical texts of modernity, however, have remained
untouched by this deconstruction. The *Meditations* are still read by most
philosophers as a series of disembodied philosophical arguments, with all the
most cherished historical clichés and sedimented emphases intact. The time
seems overdue for some fresh approaches to the *Meditations*, readings which
will incorporate and reflect our changed understanding of the modern
scientific project and the new insights made available as a result of our growing critical detachment from that project. This study offers such a reading.

Although the essays range over a variety of cultural arenas, and draw on secondary material from several disciplines, the primary focus throughout is Descartes's *Meditations*. A good deal of discussion in these pages, accordingly, is devoted to a close examination of that text.

My approach to the *Meditations*, however, differs in several respects from traditional philosophical approaches to Descartes. First, I do not believe that one can adequately identify, interpret, or appreciate philosophical arguments so long as they are viewed as timeless, culturally disembodied events in some history of "talking heads" (as Stephen Toulmin has aptly put it). Although a coherent abstract or ahistorical reading is possible, the dilemmas Descartes constructs, the solutions he embraces, make their fullest sense in the context of the cultural pressures that gave rise to them. Cartesian doubt, the Evil Genius, the *cogito*, I would insist, are more fruitfully read through the template of the cultural turmoil of the seventeenth century, and resulting historical changes in the structure of human experience, than as ever-applicable, "enduring" philosophical experiences.

The anticultural attitude runs very deep in philosophy. It has been essential to the discipline's conception of itself as "cultural overseer," able to transcend history and discover an ultimate "neutral framework" within which to situate other human endeavors or describe reality.[2] This attitude has proved increasingly difficult for philosophy to sustain in the intellectual wake of the work of Richard Rorty, Michel Foucault, and feminist historians of science and philosophy such as Sandra Harding and Evelyn Fox Keller. Philosophy has been forced to recognize that its "enduring" issues and "timeless" concerns are the products of very particular cultural circumstances. The lesson needs to be taken into the classroom, too. If we insist that students view Descartes as their contemporary, they will almost certainly see his concerns as bizarre, idiosyncratic, and obsessive — yet another confirmation of the alien nature of the philosophic mentality. In cultural context, his arguments emerge as inventive, ingenious, and often beautifully concise expressions of and strategies for dealing with cultural crisis and the need for intellectual "re-visioning." Throughout these essays, therefore, I am constantly stepping back from the text, to survey the culture in which the text is located and given body.

My interpretation of the *Meditations* is not only informed by a cultural context, but by a *psycho*cultural framework. A psychological mood has often marked recent intellectual histories and analyses of modern science and epistemology. Both Baconian empiricism and Cartesian mechanism have been explored in terms of domination, aggression, and the impulse to control

(Berman, Merchant, and Easlea). The Cartesian dream of a unified system of absolute knowledge, the ideal of a perfectly "mirrored" nature, have begun to be scrutinized from a more Nietzschean or Deweyan perspective, as reaction-formations to epistemological insecurity and uncertainty. A shadow has been exposed, a dark underside to the bold Cartesian vision: Richard Bernstein speaks of the great "Cartesian anxiety" over the possibility of intellectual and moral chaos (p. 762), Karsten Harries refers to the Cartesian "dread of the distorting power of perspective" (p. 29) and Richard Rorty (perhaps the most influential in this regard) reminds us that the seventeenth-century ideal of "mirroring" nature is also an "attempt to escape from history," culture and human finitude (p. 9). The Cartesian epistemological ideals of clarity, detachment, and objectivity, although still largely unquestioned as requirements for scientific and philosophic investigation, have been interpreted as serving an obsessive concern with purity and a corresponding desire to exorcise all the messier (e.g., bodily, emotional) dimensions of experience from science and philosophy (Keller, Lloyd, Bordo, and Wilshire). Cartesian dualism, too, has recently been redescribed in psychiatric terms, as a schizoid "false-self system" (Berman) and a pathology of "depersonalization" (Cohen).

In many of these works, such psychological categories function primarily as a suggestive motif — evocative, illuminating, and humanizing, but rarely employed systematically. The Deweyan, therapeutic mode of a powerful and influential work such as Rorty's *Philosophy and the Mirror of Nature* has made it legitimate for philosophers, once again, to talk about the history and methodology of our discipline in naturalist terms — that is, as having developed among human creatures with biological, social, and psychological inclinations — rather than as having been determined by absolute, timeless requirements of Truth, Reason, and so on. But in Rorty and others, although the mood is often therapeutic and demystifying (Rorty would call it "edifying"), the aim is not really to psychologize about the history of thought. *Philosophy and the Mirror of Nature* is a brilliant exposé and critique of the imagery that has dominated philosophy since the seventeenth century, not a psychoanalysis of that imagery.[3]

In my reading of the *Meditations*, on the other hand, I take the psychological (and often psychoanalytic) categories of "anxiety," "dread," "denial," "reaction-formation," and "escape" very seriously as hermeneutic tools, drawing freely on insights from classical psychoanalytic, object-relations, and cognitive schools of thought. These developmental insights are of unusual value in clarifying and deepening our understanding of the *Meditations* and of the Cartesian era. They provide fresh paths of access to both familiar and obscure arguments in the text of the *Meditations*. Taken together, they also coalesce into a narrative framework — a psychocultural "story" — which allows us to re-vision, interpret, juxtapose, and connect texts and events so as to reveal previously unnoticed dimensions and coherencies. That narrative framework, as I develop it in these essays, is a "drama of parturition": cultural birth out of the mother-world of the Middle Ages and Renaissance, and creation of another world — the modern.

Within the context of this "drama," I propose, the overworked *Meditations* can still yield some surprises. The "great Cartesian anxiety," although manifestly expressed in epistemological terms, discloses itself as anxiety over *separation* from the organic female universe. Cartesian rationalism, correspondingly, is explored here as a defensive response to that separation anxiety, an aggressive intellectual "flight from the feminine" into the modern scientific universe of purity, clarity, and objectivity. My focus here is on the philosophical expression of such a "flight from the feminine," rather than the more concrete, political, and institutional dimensions chronicled by a number of authors. The form of that philosophical flight, as I describe it, is a "re-birthing" and "re-imaging" of knowledge and the world as *masculine*.

Finally, my study here is frankly and explicitly a *selective* history "of the present" (as Foucault would put it), not of the past. My interest is neither in distilling the "essence" of Cartesian rationalism nor in attempting a comprehensive account of the social, political, and philosophical currents which fed it. Rather, I am interested in those facets of Cartesianism and the seventeenth century which have emerged, through the grid of the concerns and imaginative categories of the present, as now making a claim on our attention. The story I tell here is also derived from the "artifacts" of an upper-class, white, male culture — but that, after all, is the culture I am seeking to understand.

My treatment of the Cartesian corpus, too, is highly selective — drawing on Descartes's correspondence and other works, but focusing largely on certain themes in the *Meditations*. My aim is not to provide a running commentary on every argument in the text. It is the instability and transitional quality of the sixteenth and seventeenth centuries that fascinate me — not the fully formulated systems that were to emerge, but the confrontation with chaos and processes of reconstruction that gave birth to those systems. In the *Meditations*, unlike Descartes's more mature, systematic works, those processes are explicit, they are embodied in the very structure of the work, which deliberately confronts disorder in order to secure a new metaphysical

orientation. Furthermore, the *Meditations* is an intensely psychological work
(although it has rarely been read this way by professional philosophers). For,
although purposefully entertained, Cartesian scepticism is nonetheless not
fully within Descartes's philosophical control. Rather, as I will argue, the
decision to doubt, once put into effect, calls into play a spontaneous stream
of consciousness in which every attempt to assurance is answered by vacilla-
tion, hesitation, and re-questioning. It is this quality of authentic inner
dialectic that makes the *Meditations* — with its determination, if only temporary, to stay *within* confusion and contradiction — such a revealing "win-
dow" on the instabilities of the era within which Descartes is a central figure.

Although the essays in this volume are relatively self-contained and may
be read independently of each other, they also may be read as a gradually
unfolding "argument" for the psychocultural reading of the *Meditations*, and
of the seventeenth-century scientific project in general, that I have described
above as a "drama of parturition." It is my hope that the reader will come
away with a recognition of not simply the fresh perspectives that a cultural
reading can provide, but of the necessity of cultural perspective for an ade-
quate understanding of philosophical texts. The central categories that I
offer are drawn from cognitive development theory and the psychoanalytic
literature on separation and individuation. I use these categories quite differently, however, than they have been employed in some recent studies on
gender and rationality. Therefore, a few words of clarification concerning
these differences might aid in an understanding of the essays that follow.

Recently, the insights of developmental theory have been beautifully
employed in the growing feminist literature on gender and rationality. The
focus here has been on the exposure, identification, and critique of the
masculinist biases in our disciplines, professions, and sciences. The emphasis
has been on differences in the psychological development of girls and boys
and the differences in conceptions of self/other relations and cognitive style
that result from these differing developmental scenarios. In this vein, Carol
Gilligan and Evelyn Fox Keller have argued, respectively, that developmental
theory from Freud to Kohlberg and post-Cartesian science embody structur-
ings of experience, definitions of success, and hierarchies of values that reflect
a characteristically "male" course of development, as it normally proceeds in
the bourgeois, nuclear family. Both arguments rely heavily on the work of
Nancy Chodorow, who suggests that because a more rigorous individuation
from the mother is demanded of boys (as a requisite to their attaining a
"masculine" identity in a culture in which masculinity is defined in opposi-

tion to everything that the mother represents), they grow up defining achievement and measuring their own well-being in terms of detachment, autonomy, and a clear sense of boundaries between self and world, self and others. This has resulted, in our male-dominated intellectual traditions, in the fetishization of detachment and "objectivity" in ethical reasoning and scientific rationality.

Such connections — between, for example, an emphasis on autonomy and "objectivity" and the requirements of male childhood development — can only be maintained with respect to cultures whose child-rearing practices and family structures have the relevant features. We cannot connect Plato's emphasis on the transcendence of the body, for example, to distinctively male processes of individuation from the mother. For we simply do not know enough about the intimate details of the differences, if any, in the way mothers nurtured their girl and boy infants in Athens 500 B.C. Feminist scholarship, for the most part, has recognized this, although not always explicitly enough. The historically and culturally circumscribed nature of much of Chodorow's, Dinnerstein's, and Gilligan's insights is not always made sufficiently clear in their otherwise powerful analyses.

My use of developmental theory focuses, not on gender difference, but on very general categories — individuation, separation anxiety, object permanence — in an attempt to explore their relevance to existential and epistemological changes brought about by the dissolution of the organic, finite, maternal universe of the Middle Ages and Renaissance. In an important sense the separate self, conscious of itself and of its own distinctness from a world "ouside" it, is born in the Cartesian era. It is a *psychological* birth — of "inwardness," of "subjectivity," of "locatedness" in space and time — generating new anxieties and, ultimately, new strategies for maintaining equilibrium in an utterly changed and alien world. In interpreting those anxieties and strategies, I propose, much can be learned from those theorists for whom the concepts of psychological birth, separation anxiety, and the defenses which may be employed against such anxiety, are central to a picture of human development.

Such a proposal may seem grandiose, misplaced, and ahistorical. Theories of separation and individuation and cognitive development, it might be argued, belong to a peculiarly *modern* discourse, one in which the very concept of self that is nascent and still tenuous in the Cartesian era is a fully developed given and a central focus. Moreover, the dynamics of separation and individuation describe *individual* development on the level of *infant* object relations. These categories cannot be transported so glibly to describe *cultural* developments in an advanced historical era.

In response to these objections, let me make the following qualifying remarks:

First, I agree that caution must be exercised in drawing such correspondences, and I certainly do not wish to be understood as making any general theoretical claims about the relationship of phylogeny and ontogeny, or any empirical claims about the actual evolutionary progress of the species. My interest is solely in the imaginative restoration of the experience of a *particular* culture, in order to understand the emergence of certain themes and philosophical issues.

Second, far from being ahistorical, my use of these psychological categories forces us to recognize the thoroughly historical character of precisely these categories of self, innerness, subjectivity, and so on, that describe the modern sense of relatedness to the world. They do so because they do not presuppose these categories as *givens* but view them as *developed*. To be sure, the development that someone like Margaret Mahler has in mind is *individual* development. But the originally undifferentiated experience of the infant — the psychological/cognitive "state of nature" out of which we develop into fully separate, self-conscious beings — nonetheless "argues," as a horizon for the imagination, for the possibility of human modes of relatedness to the world in which separateness of self and world is less sharply delineated than they are within the Western modern norm of cognitive experience. Such modes are argued (by Berman and Barfield, among others), to have been characteristic of prescientific experience. The categories of developmental theory, employed as hermeneutic tools for understanding key texts emerging from that experience, illuminate Berman's and Barfield's arguments and underscore their importance.

The seventeenth century, in contrast to prescientific culture, seems preoccupied with firming the distinction between self and world, between knower and known. It is just such a preoccupation that feminists and others have had in mind when they have charged the objectivist modes of rationality which have dominated the Western intellectual tradition with a distinctively male cognitive style. Modern science has come especially under such scrutiny. Indeed, it has been claimed that the birth of modern science represents a decisive historical moment in this regard, a "masculine birth of time," as Bacon himself called it, in which the more "feminine" — i.e., intuitive, empathic, associational — elements were rigorously exorcised from science and philosophy. The result was a "super-masculinized" model of knowledge in which detachment, clarity, and transcendence of the body are all key requirements.

This remarkable and provocative notion — that knowledge *became* "masculinized" at a certain point in our intellectual history — suggests that it is misleading to view the history of philosophy, as some writers have (see Lloyd), as consistently and obsessively devoted to the exclusion or transcendence of the feminine. Although men have been the cultural architects of our dominant scientific and philosophic traditions, the structures they have built are not "male" in the same way in all eras and cultures — for what it has meant to *be* "male" (or "scientific") has historically and culturally varied dramatically. Although it can certainly be argued that some degree of (culturally specific) gynophobia or misogyny may be present from Plato through present-day philosophy, this does not translate into all Western male conceptions of rationality being equally grounded in disdain or extrusion of those characteristics which have been historically identified with "the feminine." Evelyn Fox Keller convincingly argues that the images, language, and principles central to the hermetic science that mechanism dethroned in the seventeenth century are precisely those traditionally associated with the feminine (knowledge as merging with rather than domination of the object, understanding as rooted in heart rather than head, participatory, nonpatriarchal language, etc.) Moreover, they were attacked as such by the opposition, who quite explicitly see themselves, in contrast, as raising "a masculine philosophy" (pp. 43–54). Medieval philosophy, too, for all its retreat from sexuality, did *not* disparage the body's role in knowledge, nor was it especially impressed with distance and detachment as paths to understanding. Rather, it is precisely *because* all that was changed by the scientific and intellectual revolutions of the seventeenth century that we can today find meaning in describing those revolutions as effecting some sort of "masculinization" of thought.

Although it only emerges explicitly in the last essay of this study, the notion of a seventeenth-century "masculinization of thought" is nonetheless one of the guiding images of the work. If it is to be taken seriously, it also poses a profound historical question, one which has not been adequately confronted in the many excellent and ground-breaking feminist texts on gender and rationality. *Why* did the dominant intellectual culture take this decisive turn in the seventeenth century? There are many paths by which such a question could be approached: economic, political, sociological, and demographic. The path taken here is through the psychocultural framework of the "drama of parturition" described earlier. The Cartesian "masculinization of thought," I will argue, is one intellectual "moment" of an acute historical flight from the feminine, from the memory of union with the maternal world, and a rejection of all values associated with it.

Despite the ultimate narrative unity of this work, the essays are nonetheless very different from each other in terms of focus, depth, and range. Essays one and five are almost exclusively textual — detailed reexaminations of Cartesian doubt and Cartesian objectivism, as they are represented in the *Meditations*. Essays two and three belong to the genre of "history of ideas" or "history of consciousness": They locate Cartesian categories within the context of general patterns of historical change in the structure of experience and thought. Essays four and six develop the psychocultural framework within which all the elements of the study, textual and historical, may ultimately be situated.

The first essay in this volume focuses on Cartesian doubt and the need to take it seriously, not merely as an initial methodological move but as a recurrent and powerful force in the *Meditations* — a demon that refuses to remain suppressed.

Essay two shifts to the cultural context of Cartesian scepticism and to the historical elements that contributed to a pervasive and perhaps unprecedented "epistemological insecurity," of which Cartesian doubt may be viewed as the philosophic crystallization. Both this and essay one set the stage for later psychocultural interpretation, in that they establish — textually in the first essay, and culturally in the second — the centrality of anxiety and disquiet as hidden psychological "truths" behind the clean, seamless surface of Cartesian order and optomism.

Essay three focuses on the categories of "innerness" or "inwardness" (and their correlative category of an "external world"), which have recently come to the forefront of philosophical discussions of the seventeenth-century "invention of the mind" (as Rorty calls it). Rorty has pointed out how deeply the imagery of interiority permeates the origins of modern philosophy: the mind as "inner arena," ideas as "inner representations," the "inner eye" of judgement, and so forth. In this essay, I suggest that this new sense of the inwardness of experience was not an invention of philosophers, but emerged within philosophy, just as it emerged within other areas in the culture, as the result of a general transformation in the human experience of relatedness to the universe. In this essay, I also draw some initial connections between this cultural emergence of inwardness and the cognitive development of the self/world distinction in the child.

Essay four is central to this study. In it, I focus on the cultural development of the human experience of *locatedness* in space and time. Comparing that development, again, with decisive moments in the perceptual/cognitive development of the child, I advance the thesis that we view the development of locatedness and inwardness as aspects of an historical process of human individuation from nature — a "drama of parturition."

As essay one focuses on Cartesian scepticism, so essay five focuses on Cartesian objectivism. In this essay, I consider the Cartesian epistemological program in some textual detail, examining the *Meditations* as incorporating rituals of purification of the mind and transcendence of nature/body. In the course of my discussion, I reconstruct the "official" philosophical birth, in the *Meditations*, of what Rorty has called the imagery of mind as "mirror of nature" — the ideal of mental purity that has dominated philosophy since the seventeenth century.

In essay six, the various textual and psychocultural threads of this study are brought together and woven into a piece, through a consideration of the "masculine" nature of the Cartesian reconstruction of thought and world, and its relation to other aspects of a seventeenth-century flight from the feminine. Finally, all these are situated within the "drama of parturition" which is the framework of this study, and the relevance of this work to current issues in gender studies and philosophy is discussed.

Chapter One

THE PERVASIVENESS OF CARTESIAN ANXIETY; OR, TAKING CARTESIAN DOUBT SERIOUSLY

> *The mind of man . . . far from the nature of a clear and equal glass, wherein the beams of things should reflect according to their true incidences, is rather like an enchanted glass, full of superstition and imposture, if it be not delivered. . . .* Bacon, *Advancement of Learning,* Book II

> *. . . when the devil himself lights all the street lamps to show everything as other than it is* — Gogol, *Nevsky Prospect*

The scientific and philosophic revolutions of the seventeenth century reconstructed the world for a culture badly in need of new imagery and new myths. The years 1400–1600, regarded by Ortega as "the greatest crisis through which the European destiny has ever passed," had left the intellectual culture "without solid ground on which to stand . . . swinging loose on its hinges" (p. 186). No longer was there one true church. Nor could there be a claim to one true culture — sensationally increased levels of exploration and commerce with other cultures had radically upset the eurocentrism that prevailed throughout the medieval era. No longer, after the telescope, could the most intimate and ubiquitous mode of human access to the world — the naked senses — be trusted. And, perhaps most disorienting, "infinity had opened its jaws" (as Arthur Koestler puts it) with Copernicus's denial of the rotation of the heavens around the earth; the snug, finite universe of the medieval imagination had been burst asunder. Where there had formerly been "a place for everything and everything in its right place," (Lewis, 206) now even the sun and earth were homeless and lost, as in Donne's famous poem.

It would be remarkable if the "new philosophy," for all its positive emphasis on reconstruction and identification with the future, did not also reflect this horizon of past disorder. In the *Meditations*, the epistemological insecurity of the Renaissance — which had been philosophically crystallized in the sixteenth-century revival of Pyrrhonian scepticism[1] — remains powerfully alive in the form of Cartesian doubt. More than merely a lingering, hollow vestige of an earlier intellectual fashion, that doubt, presented to us through the imagery of madmen's delusions, evil geniuses, and hallucinations, appears in the text as invasive, vertiginous. The most vivid moments of the *Meditations* occur in the first two Meditations, and they create a nightmare landscape not easily dispelled from the imagination. Looking freshly at the *Meditations*, one cannot help but be struck by the manifest epistemological anxiety of the earlier Meditations, and by how unresolute a mode of inquiry they embody: the dizzying vacillations, the constant requestioning of the self, the determination, if only temporary, to stay *within* confusion and contradiction, to favor interior movement rather than clarity and resolve.

All that, of course, is ultimately left behind by Descartes, as firmly as his bad dreams (as he tells his correspondent, Elizabeth of Bohemia) were conquered by the vigilance of his reason. The model of knowledge that Descartes bequeathed to modern science, and of which he is often explicitly described as the father, is based on clarity, certainty, and detachment. Yet the transformation from the imagery of nightmare to the imagery of objectivity remains unconvincing. The sense of experience conveyed by the first two Meditations — what Karl Stern has called the sense of "reality founded on uncertainty" (p. 99) — is not *quite* overcome for the reader by the positivity of the later Meditations. Descartes's critics felt this in his own time. Over and over, they raise the objection: Given the power of the first two Meditations, how can you really claim to have extricated yourself from the doubt, and from the dream?

Modern philosophy, however, has tended to minimize the scope and power of Cartesian doubt. Perhaps this shouldn't be surprising. We are, after all, the *heirs* of the Cartesian reconstruction, which quite successfully kept the epistemological demons out of the laboratory and classroom for three hundred years. The various Cartesian "proofs" (of the distinction between mind and body, that his essence is thinking, of the existence of God, etc.) have been subjected to the most rigorous scrutiny (and usually found wanting). But the psychological "heart" of the *Meditations* — the journey from doubt and despair to certainty and hope — has been kept at arm's length. Cartesian doubt, it has been argued over and over again, has no experiential base. Rather, it is entirely strategic: a "device," a "fiction," a "form of thought therapy."[2] Descartes himself, it is sometimes claimed, is not even the real subject of the therapy, but is "playing the part" of the skeptic in order to help those less able than himself to distinguish between the seemingly certain and the actually certain (Doney, 1955; Marlies). On these readings, Cartesian doubt is entirely methodical in nature, entertained to cleanse and prepare the intellect for a fresh start — a thought experiment which, although certainly of a pervasive nature, is never genuinely entertained, is never compelling in itself. "Does [Descartes] ever *really* doubt the existence of God and the world?" Kenny asks (1968, p. 21). Very few commentators have been willing to grant the possibility of an affirmative answer to this question.[3]

The scope of Cartesian doubt has been questioned, too, particularly in the 1950s, when a school of interpretation emerged which seemed to have as its subtextual goal a minimalization of the seriousness of Cartesian doubt: the so-called "memory school" (represented by Willis Doney and A. K. Stout), which argued that Descartes's need of God's guarantee is only to insure the truth of *remembered* clear and distinct perceptions. Frankfurt, who criticizes these arguments, nonetheless asserts that "the scepticism to which [Descartes] commits himself is innocuously thin and undisruptive" (1970, p. 16). Others have dismissed some of Descartes's most experientially powerful arguments — concerning sense-perception and dreaming, for example — through demonstrations of their "absurdity" or inconsistency from the point of view of contemporary philosophy and logic.[4]

There is certainly ample evidence to support a reading of Cartesian doubt as methodical. In his correspondence, in his replies to his critics, and in the *Notes Directed Against a Certain Programme*, Descartes stresses that his doubt, unlike the doubt of the true skeptic, is intended as *provisional*, espoused only with a view toward its refutation (HR, I, 448–49). In the *Principles* (HR, I, 219) and earlier, in the *Discourse*, he strongly affirms that his "design [is] only to provide himself with good ground for assurance and to reject the quicksand and mud in order to find the rock or clay" (HR, I, 99). And in the *Synopsis* of the *Meditations*, he delivers what sounds very much like an explicit statement of the "therapeutic" function of his doubt:

> But although the utility of a Doubt which is so general does not at first
> appear, it is at the same time very great, inasmuch as it delivers us from
> every kind of prejudice, and sets out for us a very simple way by which the

mind may detach itself from the senses; and finally it makes it impossible for us ever to doubt those things which we have once discovered to be true (HR, I, 140).

In addition to these statements, we have, moreover, the image Descartes himself gives, in the first paragraph of the *Meditations*, of having *waited* several years for the leisure and maturity to confront doubt about the principles upon which his beliefs rest. Surely a "real" doubt would be insidious and infectious, not to be shelved for a calmer moment.

But even if Cartesian doubt were voluntarily produced, deliberately "put on" to cleanse the mind of its habitual proclivities, this does not rule out the experiential authenticity of Cartesian scepticism. To begin with, we need to ask why the mind should require such a ferocious *purging* as Descartes attempts, in order to relieve itself of "prejudice" and reject the "merely probable." All of Descartes's metaphors for his project suggest the necessity of such a purge: He speaks of razing buildings to their foundations (*Discourse*, I, 89), wiping clean badly conceived paintings (*Search After Truth*, I, 312), overturning baskets of rotten fruit (Objections VII; II, 282). Contemporary philosophical perspectives on these metaphors have tended to dismiss them as "misconceived" and baffling. If we instead take these Cartesian images very seriously, it becomes apparent in the process just how limited analytic criticism is by its own deeply engrained and largely unexamined Cartesianism. Embodying the confident, imperturbable philosophical standpoint bequeathed to us by the Cartesian *reconstruction*, analytic criticism is unable to enter the uncertain world of Cartesian doubt.

Anthony Kenny, for example, referring to the apple basket simile, wonders why Descartes couldn't have inspected and taken out the rotten apples (faulty beliefs) one by one, rather than overturning the whole basket, as Descartes claims he has to, lest the rotten "make the rest go bad" (1968, p. 19). The more reasonable approach, Kenny tells us, would be to sort through the mind's ideas, discarding the "rotten" ones and ultimately finding oneself left with a basket of select, unblemished fruit. These perfect fruit (clear and distinct ideas) would be the foundations of knowledge. Kenny here clearly exemplifies the philosophical orientation that was Descartes's ultimate legacy: a conceptual universe of clean boundaries and discrete natures, a universe amenable to conceptual sorting. Within such a universe, the radically doubting Descartes of the first two Meditations seems deluded or obtuse. His sceptical insistence that none of one's beliefs can be certain so long as *any* are uncertain appears to Kenny simply as a misguided presupposition for which Descartes "offers no proof."

To regard Descartes's extraordinary epistemological requirement as merely an unfounded presupposition is to miss the psychological thrust of the simile and to fail to take the imagery of contamination and corruption seriously enough. To view ideas as capable of infecting each other (as Descartes does) is, first of all, to imagine them as *affecting* each other, an important detail which is missed in Kenny's reading of the simile. For the doubting Descartes of the first two Meditations, the mind is not simply a container of assorted ideas. It is, rather, a stream of consciousness, in which ideas, as they are called up or present themselves for examination, leave traces behind, plant suggestions, instill lingering doubts. The mind has a *memory*. And for Descartes, the "memory" of fallibility is corrupting and undermining. The ideas Descartes subjects to scrutiny are, after all, precisely those ideas which common sense accepts as most trustworthy. Having notic-ed the rotten core beneath the smooth surface appearance of these normally trusted beliefs, one can't simply go on confidently picking and sorting through the "apples" of knowledge. For one is no longer sure that one will be able to *tell* the rotten from the good fruit of the mind — the encounter with obscurity, ambiguity, confusion is a worm, eating away at epistemological security. The "contamination" here is purely *psychological*, of course — it is the mind's confidence in its own discriminative capacities that has been infected. What is at stake is not the trustworthiness of particular beliefs but that of our cognitive capacities themselves.

Kenny is right, of course, about Descartes's absolutism. For Descartes, there are only two possibilities: absolute certainty or epistemological chaos; that is, purity or corruption. This is not a philosophical "assumption," however, but a perspective on reality; one which, as many authors have argued, functions as a response to anxiety. When the universe becomes unmanageable, human beings become absolutists. We create a world without ambiguity in order to escape, as Dewey puts it, "from the vicissitudes of ex-perience" (1929, p. 17), to impose order on what is experienced as without organic order of its own. Similarly, the anthropologist Mary Douglas suggests that "ideas about separating, purifying, demarcating . . . have as their main function to impose system on an inherently untidy experience" (1966, p. 4).

Certainly, Cartesianism is nothing if not a passion for separation, purification, and demarcation. Later, I will further explore this quest for purity and its cultural context. For now, I would like to concentrate on the considerable level of anxiety that fuels the Cartesian search for order. The marker of that anxiety, in the *Meditations*, is Cartesian doubt — understood, however, not as a methodological assumption, but as an experiential "space" which Descartes freely enters in order to confront the extent and limits of disorder. Certainly, Cartesian doubt is deliberately entertained. But once entertained, it exerts an independent influence over the course of the *Meditations*, a serpent crawling through Descartes's attempts at discrimination among his ideas. Even at the very start of the *Meditations* the "natural attitude" of naive acceptance of one's beliefs is described as a dream from which one "fears to awaken," which requires a conspiracy with "illusion" to maintain (HR, I, 149). And Cartesian doubt, although methodical, was powerful enough to intrude on Descartes, as I will argue, at every turn in the first half of the *Meditations*, even at those junctures where commentators have viewed Descartes as discovering the utmost in certainty.

My first focus will be Descartes's famous sceptical arguments concerning dreaming and the Evil Genius, which I take to pose far more insidious and undermining a threat for Descartes than they are often taken to pose. Next, I will turn to a discussion of the scope and irrepressibility of Cartesian doubt. Neither the compelling nature of clear and distinct ideas, nor even the *cogito*, I argue, can subdue that doubt decisively. The roots of this radical scepticism, I then suggest, are to be found in Descartes's image of the mind — as providing only the most fragile and fleeting contact with the world, the most tenuous hold on the objects it surveys. Finally, I will introduce some psychological perspectives on this image of the mind, derived from the insights of developmental theory. These perspectives, which are only briefly alluded to in this chapter, will reveal their greater significance to this study as it unfolds.

DREAMING AND MYSTIFICATION

> I shall then suppose, not that God who is supremely good and the fountain of truth, but some evil genius not less powerful than deceitful, has employed his whole energies in deceiving me; I shall consider that the heavens, the earth, colours, figures, sound, and all other external things are nought but the illusions and dreams of which this genius has availed himself in order to lay traps for my credulity . . .
>
> Meditation I

That Cartesian scepticism is a confrontation with radical lack of faith in our epistemic processes is forcefully dramatized by Descartes's dream argument (where, it appears, his repressed nightmares return with a vengeance). Descartes's goal, in the argument, is to establish a continuum between the utter epistemological "entrapment" of madness and the perceptions of ordinary life. The connecting link is the state of sleep, in which even the sanest become "mad," and may imagine themselves in situations as far from reality as the perceptions of the insane in their waking moments.

Having acknowledged that, despite the deceptive nature of the senses, *some* perceptions — e.g., "that I am here, seated by the fire, attired in a dressing gown, having this paper in my hands" (HR, I, 145) — appear to be immune to doubt, Descartes immediately casts this conclusion in question. For the thought occurs to him that there are men — i.e., madmen — who could easily be sitting just as he is and honestly believe it not to be the case. And, lest he is tempted to dismiss the possibility of such experience as being only the province of madness, he remembers that time each night when "often it has happened to me that . . . I dreamt that I found myself in this particular place . . . dressed and seated by the fire, whilst in reality I was lying undressed in the bed" (HR, I, 145–6). He concludes, at this juncture, that "there are no certain indications by which we may clearly distinguish wakefulness from sleep" (HR, I, 146).

Norman Malcolm is famous for having disputed Descartes's conclusion here. One certain indication that we are awake, he insists, is if we question (or affirm) that we are asleep. The act of questioning, on Malcolm's view (and doubting, thinking, and affirming, as well) can only be made sense of as states of consciousness. And since sleeping is not a state of consciousness, it "logically" follows that is a person doubts, claims, questions, and so forth, he or she is not asleep (p. 15).[5]

To wonder whether one is (sound) asleep, Malcolm concludes, is absurd — and involves a "kind" of self-contradiction. The contradiction is the same, for Malcolm, as that involved in the joke of answering "yes" to a second party's question as to whether or not you are sound asleep. It is also similar to Wittgenstein's critique of the solipsist in the *Blue and Brown Books*: the solipsist, Wittgenstein suggests, negates his/her own position in voicing it, because to voice it is to acknowledge the existence of at least one other being — the listener (pp. 58–59).

Whatever the merits of Malcolm's view of language, it is striking that at no point does Descartes ask us to imagine situations of the sort which Malcolm claims are absurd — e.g., the situation of being asleep and doubting that one is asleep, or of being awake and wondering if one is asleep. The closest Descartes comes (to the latter) is when he remarks that his astonishment over the similarity between the dream state and the state of wakefulness is such that "it is almost capable of persuading me that I now dream" (HR, I, 146).

But to be *persuaded* that one is dreaming is not the same as *questioning* whether one is dreaming. "*Persuasio*," for Descartes, is, as we will see, precisely that state of inner thralldom which *precludes* questioning, doubting, and so forth. It is the quality of the epistemological ideal which he would like to reach — but it has a shadow side which must be confronted and exorcised before the ideal can be underwritten. That shadow side is not merely the possibility of being wrong, but of being so *mystified* that doubts, questions, and so forth, do not arise at all.

"Maybe all this is a dream?" is not the question that haunts Descartes. Rather, he is troubled by states — like madness, like dreaming — that so completely "occupy" experiential space that there is no room for questions about the correspondence of those states to reality. The dream state is convincing, *not* because it is so vivid that it simulates reality — Descartes specifically acknowledges that his remembered dream perceptions are not as clear and distinct as the ones he has while awake (HR, I, 146) — but because, for all its murkiness, it *is* "reality" for the dreamer. In this Descartes actually agrees with Malcolm: "dead to the world" sleep is something one is either *in* or *not in*, and while *in*, it is not a state which one has any distance on such that one could question the status of the world as given.

For Descartes, however, the limits of the dream state are experiential, not logical, and lack of consciousness is not the crucial issue. He could just as easily make the same points about daydreaming which is so absorbing that it renders one "dead to the world" — and he makes the same points, of course, about madness and about the possibility of deception by the Evil Genius. When Descartes remarks that "there are no certain indications by which we may clearly distinguish wakefulness from sleep," he is led to this not through remembering that he often had mistakenly *thought* "I am awake" (while really asleep) but through remembering that he often had been deceived by the *illusion* that he was awake — which is a very different thing. To think "I am awake" indeed involves asserting or representing something to oneself. To be under the illusion that one is awake involves nothing of this sort. It is just like *being* awake, except that one isn't, and this is what troubles Descartes so.

These arguments go even deeper in their scepticism than the arguments concerning the deceitfulness of sense perception, as Descartes clearly intends them to. To think that the sun is the size of a quarter and be "proved" wrong is one thing. But to have experienced something as *real* and found it to have been an illusion is another. The latter suggests that the human mind is subject to *mystification* — that it can be caught up in states absolutely compelling (because nothing experientially available while one is in the state can suggest that it is an illusion) yet representing the world in an absolutely false way. It is this fear that underlies Descartes's need to overturn and empty *all* the contents of the mind.

How can Descartes begin to trust the results of mental processes that may occur within boundaries set by illusion? Immediately after the dream argument, he considers the possibility that he *may*, "For whether I am awake or asleep, two and three together always form five, and the square can never have more than four sides, and it does not seem possible that truths so clear and apparent can be suspected of any falsity [or uncertainty]" (HR, I, 147). But if there are any truths that appear to span the dream/reality distinction, this doesn't mean that they are immune to the possibility of occurring within the realm of illusion.

For the *whole* of my existence — sleeping, wakefulness, internal certitudes, prejudices, beliefs about the external world, feelings, the sense of embodiment — may be the result of a grand demonic deception which we cannot get *beyond* to determine the true state of things. At each step of the first *Meditation*, the possible boundaries of illusion widen: at first it is only "certain persons" — the mad — who are victims; then it is every person, but only some of the time; and finally, it is everyone, all of the time, who may be the subjects of a deception so encompassing that there is no *conceivable* perspective from which to judge its correspondence with reality. The sane may have distance on the mad and the wakeful may, in retrospect, have distance on the dream, but the specter of the Evil Genius allows no distance at all. It is a specter of complete entrapment.

CLEAR AND DISTINCT PERCEPTIONS

Only God can lift the spell. In a reply to Mersenne, Descartes stressed that the knowledge of the atheist mathematician, no matter how clear and distinct, can be rendered doubtful (HR, II, 39). The atheist, for Descartes, occupies the peculiar position of one for whom the Evil Genius hypothesis and the doubt engendered by it can *never* be dispelled. This is so because the condition for dispelling the hypothesis is precisely the recognition of the existence of a veracious God.

> That an atheist can know clearly that the three angles of a triangle are
> equal to two right angles, I do not deny, I merely affirm that, on the other
> hand, such knowledge on his part cannot constitute true science, because no
> knowledge that can be rendered doubtful should be called science. Since he

is, as supposed, an atheist, he cannot be sure that it is not deceived in the things that seem most evident to him, as has been sufficiently shown; and though perchance the doubt does not occur to him, nevertheless it may come up, if he examine the matter, or if another suggests it; he can never be safe from it unless he first recognizes the existence of God (HR, II, 39).

Nor can Descartes trust himself in the face of his clear and distinct perception that "two and three together make five." That he cannot without the Divine Guarantee is clear from the following passage from the third *Meditation*:

Certainly if I judged that since such matters [e.g., that two and three make five] could be doubted, this would not have been so for any other reason than that it had come into my mind that perhaps a God might have endowed me with such a nature that I may have been deceived even concerning things which seemed to me most manifest. But every time that this preconceived opinion of the sovereign power of a God presents itself to my thought, I am constrained to confess that it is easy to Him, if He wishes it, to cause me to err, even in matters in which I believe myself to have the best evidence (HR, I, 158).

Throughout the *Meditations*, the *Discourse* and the *Principles*, the simplest mathematical and geometric operations are often called explicitly into question (HR, I, 182, 220, 101). Despite commentators' attempts to show that Cartesian doubt falls before the clarity and purity of mathematics, or is only about the reliability of memory,[6] Descartes's position on this seems clear:

... That all things that we very clearly and very distinctly conceive of are true, is certain only because God is or exists and that He is a perfect Being, and that all that is in us issues from Him ... if we did not know that all that is in us of reality and truth proceeds from a perfect and infinite Being, however clear and distinct were our ideas, we should not have any reason to assure ourselves that they had the perfection of being true (*Discourse*, HR, I, 105).

But in the dizzying world of the *Meditations*, even Cartesian doubt is unstable. Although, so long as I am Godless, I have no *reason* to be assured of the truth of my perceptions, I may nonetheless find the tendency to do so to be *irresistible*. This is not a problem with remembered perceptions; but, in the immediacy of present clear and distinct perceptions, one is unable to "prevent [oneself] from holding them to be true" (HR, I, 180).

In your second objection you say that the truth of axioms which are clearly and distinctly conceived is self-evident. This too, I agree, is true, during the time they are clearly and distinctly conceived; because our mind is of such a nature that it cannot help assenting to what it clearly conceives (Letter to Regius, May 24, 1640, PL, 73).

If one "cannot help assenting," where is the room for doubt about the truth? And, indeed, there are passages in Descartes that suggest that under such circumstances there is no room for doubt.

> To begin with, directly we think that we rightly perceive something, we spontaneously persuade ourselves that this is true. Further, if this conviction is so strong that we have no reason to doubt concerning that of the truth of which we have persuaded ourselves, there is nothing more to enquire about; we have here all the certainty that can reasonably be desired. What it is to us, though perchance some one feigns that that, of the truth of which we are so firmly persuaded, appears false to God or to an angel, and hence is, absolutely speaking, false? What heed do we pay to that absolute falsity, when we by no means believe that it exists or even suspect its existence? We have assumed a conviction so strong that nothing can remove it, and this persuasion is clearly the same perfect certitude (Reply to Objections II, HR, II, 41).

Yet doubt creeps in, through the "back door." Returning now to the letter to Regius:

> But because we often remember conclusions that we have derived from such premises without actually attending to the premises, I say that in such a case, if we lack knowledge of God, we can pretend that they are uncertain even though we remember that they were deduced from clear principles; because perhaps our nature is such that we go wrong even in the most evident matters (PL, 73–74).

The immediate apprehension of a clear and distinct idea indeed involves a state of subjective certainty. While in the present and immediate process of intuiting a clear and distinct idea, one is "persuaded" of the truth of what is intuited; "the inclination to believe what is being intuited is irresistible" (Frankfurt, in Doney, 1967, p. 213). But when the immediacy of the intuition passes, so too passes what now appears as a very slender grip on confidence in our own faculties. That confidence is sustained by a purely psychological thread — the *feeling* of conviction — which, in passing, leaves in its wake an empty space where a possible Evil Genius may intrude. The Evil Genius may make the false *feel* irresistible, so that we may "go wrong even in the most evident matters," that is, even when *persuasio* — the sense of conviction — is compelling. *While* we are so persuaded, there is no room for doubt. But recollected perceptions, even when correctly remembered to have been clear and distinct, lack the subjective quality of *persuasio*. They are disconnected, one might say, from the *felt* sense of discovery, of insight, and so can only be taken on faith.

This might be enough, if we could sustain a sense of confidence in our past insights. But we cannot; that is what the possibility of the Evil Genius personifies: a radical lack of faith in our own epistemic process. In retrospect, our past discoveries and insights now appear as *always* having been open to doubt, although not "felt" as such at the moment when their "truth" first struck us.

> Consequently, even at the moment when we deduced [our conclusions] from those [clear] principles, we did not have scientific knowledge (*scientia*) of them, but only a conviction (*persuasio*) of them. I distinguish the two as follows: there is a conviction when there remains some reasons which might lead us to doubt, but scientific knowledge is conviction based on an argument so strong that it can never be shaken by any stronger argument. Nobody can have the latter unless he also has knowledge of God (Letter to Regius, PL, 74).

The possibility that knowledge may be rendered doubtful, therefore, is as insidious as actively entertained doubt itself. In the *Regulae*, Descartes had vowed to "trust only that which is completely known and incapable of being doubted" (HR, I, 3). The latter requirement, we now can see, is not only that we should be convinced beyond a shadow of any *present* doubt, but convinced beyond the shadow of any *future* doubt as well.

COGITO ERGO SUM AND SUM RES COGITANS

In the face of such a requirement, it is clear to Descartes that the only epistemological guarantee that comes with *all* our ideas is their indubitability *as* modes of consciousness.

> Now as to what concerns ideas, if we consider them only in themselves and do not relate them to anything else beyond themselves, they cannot properly speaking be false; for whether I imagine a goat or a chimera, it is not less true that I imagine the one than the other (Meditation III, HR, I, 159).

And:

> . . . although the things which I perceive and imagine are perhaps nothing at all apart from me and in themselves, I am nevertheless assured that these modes of thought, that I call perceptions and imaginations, inasmuch only as they are modes of thought, certainly reside (and are met with) in me (Meditation III, HR, I, 157).

Such "indubitability," however, cannot get a science of the world very far. For such indubitability is a feature of conscious events insofar as they are taken just as that: events in consciousness, neither representing nor misrepresenting any other things "apart from [us] and in themselves." Descartes's search, in the second *Meditation* begins as a search for some idea — *any* idea — which guarantees more than this; that is, which insures, not only that it is a mode of consciousness, but which certifies itself in terms of correspondence with reality. By interrogating *that* idea, perhaps, he can discover what we need to look for, in all other ideas — what test they must pass if we are to trust them as representations of the world outside us.

The idea that Descartes discovers in the second Meditation is, of course, the *cogito*, which assures Descartes that there is one judgment about the nature of *things* that insures its own correspondence with external reality — one, indeed, for which the issue of correspondence between idea and reality cannot arise. That judgment is *sum*.

The indubitability of events in consciousness now plays a role in establishing the special indubitability of *sum*: Whatever I am thinking, I cannot doubt that I think. That "I think" entails "*sum*" cannot be doubted: "Of a surety I myself did exist since I persuaded myself of something" (*cogito ergo sum*). And if *cogito ergo sum*, then the truth of *sum* as a proposition cannot be doubted:

> ... let him deceive me as much as he will, he can never cause me to be nothing as long as I think that I am something ...

> I am, I exist, is necessarily true each time that I pronounce it, or that I mentally conceive it (HR, I, 150).

It is generally believed that the search for indubitability ends here, with the discovery of the *cogito*. And, indeed, the *cogito is* indubitable — but in a rather special sense, as I will argue, that precludes the possibility of abstracting *general* criteria for truth from it. In only one place, in fact, does Descartes claim that the truth of the *cogito* is assured by virtue of its "clearness and distinctness," and that is in the *Discourse*.[7] In the *Meditations* it is *sum res cogitans*, not the *cogito*, that is assured precisely by virtue "of the clear and distinct perception [which it states]" (I, 158), and from which the criteria are derived as a guide to truth. And other external evidence, too, points in the direction of *sum res cogitans* as the epistemological pivot on which the abstraction of general criteria for truth turns: In the *Synopsis* to the *Meditations*, Descartes says that the *cogito* is "of greatest moment" *because* it then allows us to draw the distinction "between things which pertain to mind ...

and those which pertain to body," that is, between *res cogitans* and *res extensa*. In a letter to Mersenne (January 1641), Descartes says that what he wants "people mainly to notice" in the second Meditation is the proof "that the human mind is better known to us than the body" (which is the title of the Meditation) (PL, 94). And in a May 1637 letter to Silhon, he says that "the *first thing* one can know with certainty" is that "[man], that is his soul, is a being or substance which is not at all corporeal, whose nature is solely to think" (PL, 34; emphasis added).

The ontological distinctness of mind and body, and the exclusion of body from the human essence, are, finally, what makes the Cartesian reconstruction of knowledge possible. The body, as we will see in more detail in essay five, is the chief impediment to human objectivity for Descartes. Here, however, *res cogitans* functions as a reassurance, not of the mind's independence from body but of the mind's ability to sort its ideas, one from the other, arriving at firm, nonambiguous distinctions. The ability to determine *sum res cogitans* proves to Descartes that the world is not a complete chaos, and that the mind is not a morass from which it is impossible to cull the firm from the rotten fruit of knowledge.

The *cogito* cannot provide such reassurance because Descartes does not arrive at it through an epistemological process of discrimination. Just what sort of truth the *cogito does* represent has been much debated among philosophers.[8] Descartes says that to doubt *cogito ergo sum* is to involve oneself in a "manifest contradiction." But, although he compares this "contradiction" to the denial that two plus three equal five (HR, I, 159), the *cogito* does not really belong even to the class of analytic truth, and the "contradictory" nature of its denial is of a special kind. Neither simply logical nor simply experiential, the indubitability of the *cogito* has to do, one might say, with (Descartes's version of) the logic of experience, in that its denial, as Bernard Williams puts it, is "*pragmatically* self-defeating."

> A logical falsehood is false in all possible states of affairs, its contradictory true in all possible states of affairs; but Descartes does not believe, either now or later in his reflections, that this thought or his existence are in any such way necessary features of the universe . . . . He might have not existed; but in any state of the world in which he did not exist, of course he could not then think, believe, assert, etc. that fact. The denials of 'I am thinking' and 'I exist' are not logical falsehoods, but pragmatically self-defeating or self-falsifying — we might compare someone's saying 'I am absent' in a roll-call (p.74).

This is a *species* of certainty, to be sure, but of a rather specialized sort (Malcolm's "I am awake," it can be seen, belongs to the same family). It cannot begin to do the work Descartes needs done. What it does do is to assure Descartes that the mystification of the mind cannot be total; it places an initial "limit," as Tweyman puts it, on the powers of the Evil Genius (p. 124): " . . . *let him deceive me as much as he will*, he can never cause me to be nothing so long as I think that I am something" (HR, I, 150; emphasis added). But the lesson of the *cogito* can have no application, for example, to judgments about external objects — which are the sorts of judgments with which Descartes is most concerned.

Sum res cogitans is important to Descartes because it establishes, not just *one* indubitable truth, but the general ability of the mind to discriminate among its ideas, to isolate those it *knows best* from those it knows only obscurely. Confirming this ability represents a much broader assault on the hypothesis of the Evil Genius, for it establishes that the faculty of the intellect itself has some artillery at its disposal. The mind is not simply a morass of ideas, for some are clear and distinct and others are obscure and confused, and they may be sorted out. *The sum res cogitans* conclusion comes at the end of the first attempt at such sorting, and it is established, not by showing that there is something peculiar about it which makes it impossible to deny (as with the *cogito*), but by discarding everything from the conception of "self" which is obscure and confused (HR, I, 152-56).

Descartes is certain, at the end of this inquiry, that his essence is thinking, and that he has been assured of this by virtue of the clearness and distinctness of the perception. But, puzzlingly, the "general rule" that he believes he may establish from this — "that all things which [are perceived] very clearly and distinctly are true" (HR, I, 158) — is still open to doubt. That doubt is "very slight, and so to speak metaphysical," but it is insidious nonetheless.

> . . . in order to be able altogether to remove it, I must inquire whether there is a God as soon as the occasion presents itself; and if I find out there is a God, I must also inquire whether He may be a deceiver; for without a knowledge of these two truths I do not see that I can ever be certain of anything (Meditation III, HR, I, 159).

Why has doubt reasserted itself? And, having discovered the possibility of achieving certainty through the mind's own operations, why Descartes's need for God's guarantee?

THE FRAGMENTARY NATURE OF THE INNER LIFE
AND THE TENUOUSNESS OF THE EXTERNAL WORLD

For Descartes no less than Berkeley, God functions as a principle of continuity beyond the discontinuities of human experience.

There are other matters that are indeed perceived very clearly by our intellect, when we attend sufficiently closely to the reasons on which our knowledge of them depends, and hence we cannot then be in doubt about them; but since we can forget those reasons, and yet remember the conclusions deduced from them, the question is raised whether we can entertain the same firm and immutable certainty as to these conclusions, during the time that we recollect that they have been deduced from first principles that are evident; for this remembrance must be assumed in order that they may be called conclusions. *My answer is that those possess it who, in virtue of their knowledge of God, are aware that the faculty of understanding given by Him must tend towards truth*; but that certainty is not shared by others (Reply to Objections II, HR, II, 42–43; emphasis added).

For Descartes, indeed, discontinuity is a central fact of human experience. Nothing — neither certainty nor temporal existence itself — endures past the present moment without God. Time — both external and internal time — is so fragmented that "in order to secure the continued existence of a thing, no less a cause is required than that needed to produce it at the first" (HR, II, 56). This means not only that our continued existence is causally dependent on God (Meditation III, HR, I, 158-9), but that God is required to provide continuity and unity to our inner life as well. That inner life, without God, "is always of the present moment" (Poulet, in McLuhan, 241); two and two may equal four *right now*, while we are attending to it, but we need God to assure that two and two will always equal four, whether we are attending to it or not (Tlumak, 62). Only God can provide what Kenny calls "the immutable state of mind" (1968, p. 92). The alternative would be a constant state of mental vigilance, a perpetual confrontation and interrogation of each idea that presents itself to us — a requirement that would make scientific progress impossible.

Metaphysical doubt, says Alexander, is "doubt by inattention," a "neurotic fear" that without a veracious God to hold our intuitions "steady," the human intellect would have nothing to ground itself on but the most fleeting of certainties (p. 121). The sense of the *fragility* of our cognitive contact with the world is so strong in Descartes that passing "second thoughts" about a matter once decided are enough to topple the most rigorously argued conclusions.

For although I am of such a nature that as long as I understand anything very clearly and distinctly, I am naturally impelled to believe it to be true, yet because I am also of such a nature that I cannot have my mind constantly fixed on the same object in order to perceive it clearly, and as I often recollect having formed a past judgment without at the same time

properly recollecting the reasons that led me to make it, it may happen
meanwhile that other reasons present themselves to me, which would easily
cause me to change my opinion, if I were ignorant of the facts of the existence of God, and thus I should have no true and certain knowledge, but
only vague and vacillating opinion (Meditation V, HR, I, 183–4).

The sense conveyed in the above quotation — of the utter impermanence
of all mental states, and of the impossibility of securing a firm foundation
for any one of them — is arresting. If the "other reasons" in the above quotation are not based on attention to the object (and so, could not be clear and
distinct), why should they so "easily cause me to change my opinion"? At
most, one feels, they might suggest the appropriateness of a rethinking of the
matter at issue, a retracing of the investigation. And why should the
possibility that past discoveries may be in error entail the possibility that *all*
opinion is "vague and vacillating"?

   The question posed above can be approached as requiring a purely
philosophical answer — in which case Descartes can provide no "justification" for his absolutist criteria for certainty. But it may also be approached
as an historical question — as I will deal with it in the next chapter, through
a brief consideration of the cultural sources of epistemological insecurity in
the Cartesian era. It may also be approached *psychoculturally*, as pointing in
the direction of an historical experience of self and world which we may have
difficulty "entering" empathically — because it is no longer our own. But
although we cannot *experience* the world of pre-Modernity, we *can*
reconstruct it in the imagination. The tools at our disposal are various: art,
literature, language, and the cultural "artifacts" of the era in question. A
suggestive analogy, moreover, can be drawn to another world which we
cannot enter — the experience of the developing child.

   That experience, as we learn from both cognitive psychology and
psychoanalytic thought, begins as an undifferentiated continuum between
child and world. (The "world," at the earliest stages of development, is, of
course, the mother; later, as the child begins to interact more actively and
extensively with the environment, other people and things are included in
the horizon of world.) The child originally does not distinguish between its
impulses, perceptions, emotions, and actions and events occuring external
to it — there is no construction of "inner" and "outer," no sense of "I," no
perception of experience as bounded by a *self*. The "normal" course of
development — both cognitive and emotional — leads away from this state
of subject/world union toward the structuring of an increasingly more

discrete "self" and an increasingly more distinct "external world." ("Normal" here of course refers to what is normal within a Western, modern context, since that is the context within which such observations have been made.) The process, looked at in general terms, has two reciprocal "moments": The child disentangles herself from the world, and the world becomes ever more "de-subjectified," or *objective*.

The process has emotional and cognitive consequences of decisive impact, which will prove relevant to this study. For now, let us only consider the course of cognitive development. From Piaget we learn that the earliest perceptions of objects, as the child begins to develop out of the original state of absolute continuity between self and world, last only as long as the infant's immediately present sensory contact with things. The mother's face "exists" for the child only so long as the mother is visually present. When she leaves the perceptual field, the child's attention and interest rapidly wane. The child thus does not at first perceive objects as having enduring stability, provided by the object's continuing existence, irrespective of the child's perception. Rather, the object-world is characterized by "continuous annihilations and resurrections," depending upon whether or not the object is within the child's perceptual field. When an object leaves the child's sight, it (effectively) leaves the universe (Piaget, 1954, 1967). Later, as the sense of "permanent object concept" develops, the child will begin to search for absent objects, indicating the development of the child's awareness of a stable, objective existence of external things, which is impervious to the vicissitudes of the child's subjective connection with them.

Consider now Descartes's concern over the inability of the mind to be "constantly fixed on the same object in order to perceive it clearly" (and thus, without God's guarantee, to be assured only of "vague and vacillating opinion"). The implicit model of absolute epistemological security here (which Descartes knows cannot be fulfilled — thus, the need for God) seems to require a constant state of mental vigilance over the object; in the absence of that, nothing can be certain. To put this in more concrete terms: No previously reached conclusions, no past insights, no remembered information can be trusted. Unless the object is present and immediately "in sight," it ceases to be available to the knower.

Descartes's epistemological instability — absolute assurance in the immediate presence of the object and absolute abandonment in its absence — is structurally very like that of the developing child's. This is not to say that Descartes saw the world as a child does. He, of course, *had* "permanent object concept." In speaking of perceiving "objects" he is not talking about rudimentary perception, but of the intellectual apprehension of the essences of things. But there is a suggestive analogy to be drawn here between his "doubt by inattention" and the perceptual deficiencies of the developing child. That analogy allows us to begin to enter the world of the *Meditations* empathically, and to move beyond our modern sense of bafflement at the seeming seriousness with which Descartes entertained his radical doubt.

What is suggested, perhaps — and it is a suggestion that will be explored throughout this study — is an experience of the world which was far more tenuously grounded in the distinction between subject and object, between self and world, than our modern adult "norm" of experience. The limits of self and world, rather, come and go; the sense of a stable, enduring world and a stable, enduring inner life surfaces, then recedes. This is the picture which Descartes presents at the start of the *Meditations*. Within its precarious sense of reality, as I have argued, not only certainty but *doubt* is unstable, ephemeral. Permanence and security, in such a world, require "holding things down," keeping constant track of the maddeningly undependable, now-present, now-absent object.

At the same time, we must recognize that in the modern era, and in the work of Descartes in particular, we witness precisely that final detachment of self and world, that firming of the distinctions between inner and outer, between mental and physical, that were to dominate philosophical imagery and argumentation for the next three hundred years. Neither of these "readings" excludes the other or is to be reduced to the other. Rather, the construction of an intellectual framework which can admit these seemingly paradoxical currents in Descartes, and find meaning in their cultural emergence in the seventeenth century, is the task of this study.

Chapter Two

THE EPISTEMOLOGICAL INSECURITY OF THE CARTESIAN ERA

> *When [the] world had itself been transformed by Galileo and his colleagues, what had seemed so simple and natural took on the aspect of a mystery. In the new world their renderings of knowledge appeared no longer as statements of a fact, but as posing of a problem. Fresh knowledge made knowledge itself seem impossible in the world it purported to describe.*
>
> John Herman Randall,
> *The Career of Philosophy*

The deceptiveness of the senses sounds the first note in what will become a full symphony of doubt in the first Meditation.

> All that up to the present time I have accepted as most true and certain I have learned either from the senses or through the senses; but it is sometimes proved to me that these senses are deceptive, and it is wiser not to trust entirely to anything by which we have once been deceived (HR, I, 145).

As various commentators have pointed out, this seems a radical conclusion. Why should the fact that we have *sometimes* been deceived by the senses lead us to withhold *all* trust in the senses? If we have only *sometimes* been deceived, then it should follow that we have not *always* been deceived. Moreover, the discovery of deception — e.g., that the sun is larger than it looks to the naked eye — is a *correction* of perception, and, as Kenny argues, "if sense perceptions can be corrected, there must be some reliable sense perceptions to set the standard by which the correction is to be made" (1968, p. 25). Walsh makes a related point.

Suppose it were indeed the case that not one of our perceptual experiences could not be warranted as reliable: we should never be in a position to say that we are sometimes deceived by our sense judgments, for in the circumstances envisaged we should not know what it was not to be so deceived. In order to decide that we were mistaken on a particular occasion we need to be able to contrast the experience we had then with others which we take to be nondeceptive; if no sense experience can be taken as being in order the contrast cannot be made (p. 91).

These rejoinders to Descartes seem well-taken and reasonable. In fact, they are too reasonable. To treat the content of the *Meditations* noncontextually, as a series of arguments which stand or fall under the scrutiny of contemporary philosophy, is to fail entirely to enter the thought-world of the first Meditation. For in that world, like the era in which Descartes lived, nothing is "reliable" or "in order," least of all sense experience.

In the previous essay, taking Descartes's own images very seriously, and following the vacillations of the text through all its dizzying turns, I attempted to recreate a sense of the unstable and precarious world of the *Meditations*. The essay may be understood, loosely, as a "phenomenology" of Cartesian scepticism. In the present essay, I will turn to the historical context of that scepticism. It is only in such context that Cartesian doubt concerning the senses, and, more radically, concerning the human mind, becomes fully comprehensible. Failure to attend to that context, accordingly, can result in a shally philosophical understanding of the *Meditations*.

Descartes begins his critique of the senses by mentioning sense-deceptions "concerning things which are hardly perceptible, or very far away" (HR, I, 145). Later in the *Meditations*, Descartes provides a specific example of this: the perception that the "sun [is] extremely small." This misleading "idea" of the sun, indeed, "derives its origin in the senses" (Meditation III, HR, I, 161). But the means of its *correction* — astronomical reasoning — is not itself a more reliable sense perception. On the contrary, according to Burtt, it represents "the supreme example of the victory of mathematics over the senses" (p. 79). Burtt here echos, although with less approval, Galileo's famous appraisal of Copernicus's discoveries as "[committing] such a rape upon the senses" that he (Galileo) can only stand in awe of the man who perservered in holding to them (Koyré, 90).

Turning to the cultural context of the *Meditations*, we should take the violence of Galileo's imagery very seriously. In "raping" the senses, Copernicus (and Galileo even more so) had destroyed one of the pivots upon which the epistemological security of the Middle Ages had turned. "Knowledge is not a problem for the ruling philosophy of the middle ages," says Burtt; "That the whole world which man's mind seeks to understand is intelligible to it was explicitly taken for granted" (p. 16). Commentators have pointed to various reasons for this confidence,[1] but central among them is surely the esteemed place granted to sense-experience in the pursuit and acquisition of "this-worldly" knowledge (and, ultimately, through such knowledge, to knowledge of God and the world beyond the mundane). Throughout the Middle Ages the idea is kept alive, according to Lovejoy, "that the world of temporal and sensible experience is . . . the supreme manifestation of the divine" (p. 97). Other commentators disagree with such emphasis on the continuities between the "this-worldly" and the "other-worldly," but most seem to agree that at least as concerns knowledge of "this-world," sensible experience was regarded as a trustworthy guide, as it had been for Aristotle.

For Aristotle, says Marjorie Grene, "what is first for us is the concrete object grasped in sense perception; through analyzing out its essential character we arrive . . . at the more difficult grasp of first principles appropriate to . . . scientific knowledge" (p. 71). So for the medievals, that which appeared different to the senses — e.g., water, ice, steam — were regarded *as* actually different. And substances, accident, matter, essence, form — the medieval categories of scientific description of the world (as contrasted with the modern categories of time, space, energy, and mass) — seem perfectly "developed to put into scientific form the facts and relations observed in man's unaided sense experience in the world" (Burtt, 18).

Although it is with Aristotle that sense-perception is dignified not only as a "delight" but as a necessary step to knowledge of the stable and universal, even for Plato it is never a mere illusion, never a "deception." Although sensation cannot yield knowledge, which is by definition of the unchanging, it nonetheless leads us quite reliably *outside ourselves* — to the sensible, changing physical world itself.

In the *Theatetus*, for example, Protagoras is criticized for the view that perception is knowledge, but he is appreciated for recognizing that man is, indeed, "the measure of all things" as regards the world of "becoming." Perception is, indeed, infallible there, and not just in the limited Cartesian sense in which all perceptions *as* perceptions are indubitable. Perception is defended on metaphysical grounds:[2] Insofar as we are dealing with perception, Plato suggests, there are, indeed, different "becomings" for different perceivers. But the conclusion to be drawn from this is not that perception is "relative." For these "becomings" do not occur simply on the side of the subject, but "in the space between" sense organ and object, through an "intercourse" that "gives birth" to, for example, colors, hot, hardness, and so on. "Transcience" and "relativity" are here qualities in the world of appearance.

> The conclusion from all this is . . . that nothing is one thing just by itself, but is always in the process of becoming for someone, and being is to be ruled out altogether (157b).

Although the argument will, as Cornford says, "prove fatal to the claim of perception to be knowledge of true reality," it also establishes that the objects of perceptions, since they are in part dependent on the perceiver to *become*, can never be "misrepresented" by the perceiver.

One thing that is striking about this view in comparing it, for example, with Galileo's distinction between primary and secondary qualities is that what Plato believed to take place in sense-perception is looked to as informative: The typical human process of perceiving is not taken as suspect, but as a norm of one of the ways human beings make contact with the world. Looking at the process of sense-perception reveals something about the *world* of "becoming," it is a "clue" to metaphysical distinctions. For Galileo, reason is the only guide for making any such distinctions, and the senses impede its progress.

> Now . . . whenever I conceive any material or corporeal substance, I immediately feel the need to think of it as bounded, and as having this or that shape; as being large or small in relation to other things, and in some specific place at any given time; as being in motion or at rest; as touching or not touching some other body; and as being one in number, or few, or many. From these conditions I cannot separate such a substance by any stretch of my imagination. But that it must be white or red, bitter or sweet, noisy or silent, and of sweet or foul odor, my mind does not feel compelled to bring in as necessary accompaniments. Without the senses as our guides, reason or imagination unaided would probably never arrive at qualities like these. Hence I think that tastes, odors, colors, and so on are no more than mere names so far as the object in which we place them is concerned, and that they reside only in consciousness . . . if the living creature were removed, all these qualities would be wiped away and annihilated (p. 274).

Gone is the notion of a "space between" the organs of perception and the object. In its place is a space "inside" the subject which stands between the subject and the world. Secondary qualities "belong entirely to us": touch resides "in the palms of the hands and in the fingertips," "heat belongs . . . ultimately to us," "sensations . . . have no real existence save in us" (pp. 275–77). So, too, for Descartes:

... although in approaching fire I feel heat, and in approaching it a little too near I even feel pain, there is at the same time no reason in this which could persuade me that there is in the fire something resembling this heat any more than there is in it something resembling the pain; all that I have any reason to believe from this is, that there is something in it, whatever it may be, which excites in me these sensations of heat or of pain (Meditation VI, HR, I, 194).

What has happened here is something Sterling Lamprecht pointed out (p. 220) long before Rorty illuminated it in the context of "the invention of the mind": "Appearances" — which for the Greeks had comprised a *world*, about which the senses are ideally suited to provide information — have been transformed into mental states, related to the world only causally. It is in these mental states that we find the stuff of error.

[Although the ideas based on sense experience] did proceed from objects different from myself, it is not a necessary consequence that they should resemble these. On the contrary, I have noticed that in many cases there was a great difference between the object and its idea. I find, for example, two completely diverse ideas of the sun in my mind; the one derives its origin from the senses, and should be placed in the category of adventitious ideas; according to this idea the sun seems to be extremely small; but the other is derived from astronomical reasonings, i.e. is elicited from certain notions that are innate to me, or else it is formed by me in some other manner; in accordance with it the sun appears to be several times greater than the earth. These two ideas cannot, indeed, both resemble the same sun, and reason makes me believe that the one which seems to have originated directly from the sun itself, is the one which is most dissimilar to it (Meditation III, HR, I, 161).

The relocation of tastes, colors, odors, and so forth, on the side of the subject brings to the subject all those qualities previously associated with the world of appearance. There is now a human capacity which, rather than being suited to apprehend a world of transient reality, is *itself* a world of transient reality: fluctuating, relative, and impermanent.[3]

It is hard to overestimate, I believe, the crisis in intellectual confidence that must have occurred when faith in the senses came to be seen as an impediment to an understanding of the world. Even for Plato, the senses had been *informative* — not of the "real," of course, but of the visible world of phenomena, with which the senses are uniquely suited to make contact. After Galileo, the results of such contact — tastes, colors, odors, tones, heat, cold — "are no more than mere names so far as the object in which we place them is concerned." They "reside only in consciousness," says Galileo (p.

274), and to think otherwise, as we shall see, is for Descartes one of the most dangerous errors of the intellect.

One must appreciate, too, the epistemologically undermining effect of the Reformation crisis, which Richard Popkin has described as contributing to a "total *crise pyrrhonienne*" in the seventeenth century (p.54). The religious crisis is of special importance in connection with Descartes, for the authority of inner conviction — precisely the extraordinary new notion of "religious evidence" advanced by Luther and Calvin — is also *the* central philosophical issue for Descartes.

Persuasio without God, as we have seen, is not enough for Descartes. Although clear and distinct perceptions are "irresistible," unless we can be assured that this subjective response to them is a mark of their *truth* (e.g., that God has made us such that we will not find the false irresistible), we remain without "true science." This does not mean, however, that Descartes is searching for some *basis* other than conviction with which to ground knowledge. The problem, rather, as I will argue later, is to "ground" conviction itself, so that we may trust the ideas that have aroused it, even after the subjective "moment" of conviction passes. It is not until after the fourth Meditation that Descartes believes he has accomplished this. Descartes's pyrrhonian critics in his own time, however, remained skeptical, throwing back at Descartes his own radical doubt in the earlier Meditations, and emphasizing, in particular, the *vicissitudes* of conviction, and the contradictory consequences of trusting to them.

> . . . since you are not ignorant of the argument of the Skeptics, tell me what else can we infer to be true as being clearly and distinctly perceived, except that which appears to anyone does appear. Thus it is true that the taste of a melon appears to me to be of this precise kind. But how shall I persuade myself that therefore it is true that such a savour exists in the melon? When as a boy and in enjoyment of good health, I thought otherwise, indeed, perceiving clearly and distinctly that the melon had another taste. Likewise, I see that many men think otherwise also, as well as many animals that are well equipped in respect of the sense of taste and are quite healthy . . . . Practically the same account must be given to those things that are relative to the mind. I could have sworn at other times that we cannot pass from a lesser to a greater quantity without passing through the stage of equality (to a fixed quantity): that two lines which continually approach one another cannot fail to meet if produced to infinity. I seemed to myself to perceive those truths so clearly and distinctly that I took them for the truest and most indubitable of axioms: nevertheless arguments subsequently presented themselves which convinced me of the opposite, seeming to make me perceive that more clearly and more distinctly . . . . You yourself indeed

experience this difficulty, because previously you admitted many things to be altogether certain and manifest, which you afterwards discovered to be dubious (Gassendi Objections, HR, II, 151-2; see also Mersenne Objections, HR, II, 27; Hobbes Objections, HR, II, 75).

The variability of conviction is a prominent theme, too, in the writing of Montaigne.

> How diversely we judge things! How many times we change our notions! What I told today and what I believe, I hold and believe it with all my belief; all my tools and all my springs of action grip this opinion and sponsor it for me in every way they can. I could not embrace or preserve any truth with more strength than this one. I belong to it entirely, I belong to it truly. But has it not happened to me, not once, but a hundred times, a thousand times, and every day, to have embraced with these same instruments, in this same condition, something else that I have since judged false (in Frame, 223-35)?

And it was an argument that was raised against the reformers, who found themselves within the same sort of circle that Descartes was charged with. We may trust our strongest convictions if we are truly in touch with God, says Luther, because the Holy Ghost has "inscribed them in our hearts." How do we know that we are in touch with God? — through the light of our inner conviction (Popkin, 10).

Descartes's proposed "grounding" for conviction, as we will see in essay five, is more complicated than this and was not fully understood by his skeptical critics. But it was the Reformation, and the cultural and scientific upheavals of the sixteenth and seventeenth centuries, that pressed the project on Descartes. Those upheavals resulted in the ascendancy of new sets of beliefs about the nature of the universe and the human being's place within it — and they did so, not simply through undermining a set of old beliefs, but by throwing into question the very status of belief and the possibility of adjudicating among beliefs. This, as we have seen, is the nature of the anxiety underlying Descartes's "apple basket" simile — that there is no ultimate grounding for human discrimination, for sorting the rotten from the good apples of knowledge.

As an example of the effect of cultural transformation on epistemology and what it views as "problems," take the new "inner criterion" of religious knowledge. On the one hand, it was just that — a new criterion. But at the same time (as Popkin persuasively argues) it was in the nature of that criterion that it ultimately cast doubt on the possibility of any criterion being guaranteed. So long as the authority of doctrine was unquestioned, this was simply not an issue. But with two criteria in conflict, how was one to decide, other than through appeal to principles already assumed in the criterion (e.g., "inner persuasion" or "the authority of doctrine") or through a pyrrhonian skepticism such as Erasmus's (e.g., given the impossibility of guarantee for one's beliefs, why not simply accept the Church?) (Popkin, 6).

As another example, take the discovery of a previously unknown and radically different culture. Such a discovery *could* be taken as demanding an enlarged or amended conception of human nature (if one were willing to accept the alien culture as "human," of course). But precisely to the degree that it appears strange or alien and *itself* based on a different *conception* of human nature, it also raises the possibility of the radical *relativity* of such conceptions. This issue began to fascinate and to trouble intellectuals in the sixteenth and seventeenth centuries. Joined with a rising awareness and interest in spatial perspective,[4] the discovery of undreamed of lands and cultures seriously raised the possibility that the "point of view," rather than the intelligible order of the universe, is the guiding force behind human belief.

The theme is prominent in the writings of Montaigne. In "Of Coaches," he moves swiftly from a consideration of "the perpetual multiplicity and ever-changing vicissitudes of forms" within the human world to the notion that our knowledge must, of necessity, present a "false image" of things.

> How vainly do we nowadays conclude the decline and decrepitude of the world by the fond arguments drawn from our own weakness, drooping and decline . . . . And as vainly did another conclude its birth and youth, by the vigour he perceived in the wits of his time, abounding in novelties and invention of divers arts (in Ross and McLaughlin, 158).

For Montaigne, we are bound by the limits of our "point of view." And although the "point of view of others can be imaginatively reconstructed, that reconstruction, for him, only serves to underscore the perspectivity of human thought. A little later in "Of Coaches" is a striking passage, in which Montaigne imagines, from the point of view of the "savage" of the "New World," how the Europeans must have appeared.

> . . . the just astonishment which those nations might justly conceive by see-ing so unexpected an arrival of bearded men, divers in language, in habit, in religion, in behavior, in form, in countenance, and from a part of the world so distant and where they had never heard there was any habitation;
> mounted upon great and unknown monsters against those who had never so much as seen a horse and less any beast whatsoever apt to bear or taught to carry either man or burden; covered with a shining and hard skin and

armed with slicing-keen weapons and glittering armour against them who for the wonder of the glittering of a looking-glass or of a plain knife would have changed or given inestimable riches in gold, precious stones and pearls (in Ross and McLaughlin, 160).

The passage is ironic, of course, forcing a recognition on the part of the European reader of just how culture-bound, how "subjective," the initial European perception of the inhabitants of the New World was. For almost every ingredient of the description — the strangeness of the new people, the geographical ignorance of the reaches which are their home, the "monsters" which reside there — corresponds to the initial European perspective on the New World. We need to put ourselves "inside" the experience of others to understand how they "see" the world, Montaigne is telling us. Once inside, we will be forced to recognize just how deeply "inside" our own experience we always and finally are. One's culture, Europe was learning, is a major determinant of that experience. The disturbing implication: Perhaps *everything* — perceptions, ideas, values — is determined by the vicissitudes of cultural "perspective." For "each man calls barbarism whatever is not his own practice . . . indeed it seems that we have no other test of truth and reason than the example and pattern of the opinions and customs of the country we live in" (in Frame 89).

This sort of thinking, as J.R. Hale argues, represents a radically new appreciation of the epistemological implications of cultural difference. What had brought it about was the textual recovery and "imaginative rehabilitation" (1967, p. 335) of the Ancient World, but more significantly, the geographical enlargement of the world through discovery and commerce, "the sensationally rapid opening of the aperture through which Europeans looked at their world" (Hale, 1968, p. 7).

That enlargement was so swift and formidable that it might almost be looked upon as the "material" counterpart of the infinitization of the universe. In 1490, the "known" world (known to Europeans, that is!) was essentially the same as that described by Ptolemy over twelve hundred years earlier; by 1521, the globe had been circumnavigated and a ship had sailed in every ocean (Chamberlin, 23). By the end of the sixteenth century, the world map was not radically different from that which we use today (Hale, 1968, p. 7).

It is important to remember that the new contact with other cultures included not just the "discovery" of the North American "savages," about whose status as humans the earliest explorers were confused and ambivalent (Hale, 1967, pp. 338–41), but aquaintance with the sophisticated civilizations of South America and the advanced learning of the Arabs and Chinese. Increased contact with the Chinese, in particular, upset the eurocentrism which had gone unquestioned until the fifteenth and sixteenth centuries.[5]

Hale suggests that it was contact with such cultures, combined with the reports of settlers, administrators, and missionaries in the New World (who, after all, had to become more intimate with the language and culture of the inhabitants than the initial explorers) that led to the new understanding of cultural difference. At first perceived as merely picturesque (or monstrous, or fantastical), the "strange humors, sundry sects, varying judgements, diverse opinions, different laws and fanatical customs" came to be seen, by the end of the sixteenth century, "as the products of a specific environment," a sub-ject for anthropology (1967, p. 342).

Hale points, for example, to the difference in "mental habit," as he calls it, revealed in the difference between Marco Polo's appreciation of the "Euro-pean" modesty and decorum of Cathayan women, and Covilhan's contrast between the "true modesty of a naked Brazilian girl and the false modesty of the overdressed women of fashion at home" (1967, p. 335). The difference between the two, he suggests, is not simply a difference in attitude toward the European norm (although it is clearly that too) but rather that Covilhan, unlike Polo, has come to appreciate the notion of the "cultural norm" itself. There is no longer one notion of "modesty" by which all cultures are judged; rather, there are different notions, peculiar to the particular cultures in which they arise, and embedded in them.[6] "There is nothing just or unjust," says Pascal, "but changes color as it changes climate. Three degrees of latitude upset the whole of jurisprudence and one meridian determines what is true" (p. 68). This "compare and contrast" thinking is contrasted by Hale to medieval "associational" thinking, which works with categories that unite rather than render things distinct (1967, p. 342). The new anthropological consciousness is present in Descartes's writing. In the *Discourse*, he muses:

> I also considered how very different the self-same man, identical in mind and spirit, may become, according as he is brought up from childhood amongst the French or Germans, or has passed his whole life amongst Chinese or cannibals. I likewise noticed how even in the fashions of one's clothing the same thing that pleased us ten years ago, and which will perhaps please us once again before ten years are passed, seems at the pres-ent time extravagant and ridiculous. I thus concluded that it is much more custom and example that persuade us than any certain knowledge (HR, I, 90–91).

Under such circumstances, the sense of personal conviction might indicate nothing more epistemologically trustworthy than the power of upbringing. And, if this is true, then epistemological certainty is sustainable only through a sort of bad faith. The "bad faith" required is that one should ignore an epistemological abyss (relativism, perspectivism, the problem of justifying criteria of discrimination, etc.) which has undeniably opened up. This is the "conspiracy with illusion" that Descartes, at the end of Meditation I, says is required to sustain the "natural" inclination to nonscepticism *when it is no longer natural* (when one has become theoretically sophisticated about the problem of justifying belief). So long as one is theoretically naive, to be sure, scepticism may well function therapeutically as an antidote to prejudice and custom; once *really* entertained, it becomes an actual horror to reckon with. The point of the first Meditation is to lead us from the "natural attitude" to full confrontation with this horror. That is why, if at first the "sceptical attitude" needs "careful holding in mind," by the end of the Meditation we require a "conspiracy with illusion" to maintain the *natural* attitude (HR, I, 149).

A new epistemological sophistication, paradoxically (or perhaps, naturally), is at the heart of Cartesian anxiety that even the best, most rigorous uses of our cognitive capacities may not suffice. Our very nature may be such that it has no means of separating the "rotton" from the "good" apples of knowledge, to use Descartes's homey metaphor. Faith in our convictions — our "natural" adjudicators — has been undermined by the possibility that those convictions are *merely* subjective responses: fragmented and fleeting within the individual, varying from person to person and culture to culture. Faith in the senses — the most direct and ubiquitous route of access between person and world — has been overthrown by the view that colors, tastes, hot, and cold are *merely* subjective occurrences, offering no reliable information about the world outside the subject. And faith in the capacity of the intellect to discriminate *between* the merely subjective and the objective state of things has yet to be born. Descartes, of course, was to be its father.

Well might Descartes have wondered whether the human being, as knower, is "attuned to God's will" (Harries, 36). "Man is nothing but a subject full of natural error that cannot be eradicated except through grace," despaired Pascal (p. 42). And what better image to capture the possibility that grace may not be forthcoming than the specter of an Evil Genius, powerful enough to have created us, but malicious enough to have created us with "such a deceptive nature that even the best evidence is not good enough" (Alexander, 113)? The state is indeed one of epistemological *fallenness*, from which we can only be delivered, for Descartes, through reassurance that this is God's world and we His creatures.

Chapter Three

THE EMERGENCE OF INWARDNESS

COGNITIVE DEVELOPMENT AND THE HISTORY OF CONSCIOUSNESS

The "discoveries" discussed in the previous essay represent, on a cultural level, the death of a naive, egocentric relationship between self and world. The loss of faith in the senses signals the recognition of a breach between body and world that had not existed for the medievals, for whom the body was regarded as a quite dependable epistemological guide (even if, in its sexual aspect, it was an impediment to spiritual progress). For Descartes and Galileo, what one smells, sees, hears, tastes, and touches can no longer be taken as a bridge to the world. That naive connection has snapped, decisively.

The recognition of cultural difference, even more profoundly, is nothing less than the discovery of the *Other*, and the Other's claims to independence and legitimacy. Such a discovery, as Montaigne satirically underscores, can come as quite a shock. One (read: one's culture) is no longer the sole maker of the world, the sole bestower of meaning. One is forced to reckon with the fact that there are other perspectives on things. At the same time, one is made forcefully aware, through the discovery of other perspectives, of one's own subjectivity, which emerges, for the first time, as a distinct point of view on the world. The consciousness of "Otherness," as Mead, Lacan, and

Merleau-Ponty have emphasized, makes possible the consciousness of self.

For children, as we know from Piaget, strikingly similar "moments" are part of the individual developmental process that culminates in the aquisition of "objectivity." That development, as I have described it earlier, is from an *egocentric*[1] state, in which the self and world exist on an unbroken continuum and the child does not distinguish between events occuring in the self and events occuring in the world, to one in which the sense of a mutually juxtaposed self and world is distinct, firm, and stable. The two dimensions are reciprocal: As the self becomes more discrete, so does all that lies "outside" the self.

Active exploration of the physical environment is central to this development. Through such sensori-motor exploration the child learns what remains constant and what is affected by personal activity — where the limits of personal action and power leave off and the resistance of the external world begins. The social world, too, plays a role in this process. Learning that other people — especially the mother — are separate, that they have will, plans, and desires of their own, is essential to the child's gradual recognition that she or he is not the whole world, that there are other beings which exist independently of one's wishes, and sometimes thwart them.

Interaction with a social world, with a world of others, is also required for conceptual development to take place — that is, for the child to begin to be able to mentally represent objects *in thought*, in their physical absence. "Reflection," Piaget says, "is internalized social discussion" (1968, p. 40). This is true, not only for inner conversational musing, but, more profoundly, for the inner representation of objects. To be able to mentally represent an object in its absence is to conceive of the object as constituted not by this or that transitory perception of it by the subject, but as sustained by a projected multiplicity of perspectives — as having a "being-for-others." The recognition that the world is a shared social world, that there are a diversity of perspectives to be taken on things, and that they are all perspectives on the "same" object, is, for Piaget, crucial to the full development of objectivity.

Correspondences between childhood cognitive development and the history of culture do not establish a definitive relationship between phylogeny and ontogeny. For Piaget, however, they are striking enough to suggest the validity of at least one central generalization: The movement away from egocentrism, he argues, is a developmental path common to both individual and species development.[2] Piaget frequently compares, for example, the Copernican revolution to the characteristic childhood discovery — at about eight years — that the earth moves around the sun. He views the history of ideas from the Copernican revolution on in terms of a gradual but inexorable erosion of the belief that the human being is the center of the universe. This corresponds, for Piaget, to the child's developing recognition that one's own actions do not magically sustain the universe, but that the universe has its own laws, which regulate everything in it — the recognition, for example, that the moon is not actually following the child simply because that is the way it appears, as one walks along, looking at it. The discovery of the perspectivity of human perception and cognition is a pivotal historical "moment" in Piaget's "developmental theory of ideas" (as he calls it), as it is in his theory of child development. Kant's contribution — the notion of the human mind as actively structuring rather than passively reflecting nature — is regarded by Piaget as decisive to this development in the history of ideas. It is certainly possible to see in Kant's thought, ahistorical as it is, an opening onto the more perspectivist and historicist understanding of knowledge that begins to develop in the nineteenth and twentieth centuries.

Piaget's "developmental theory of ideas" is just that — a theory of *ideas*. The parallels he draws are between child development and historical *belief* systems, as crystallized in the formal theories of philosophers and scientists. Those beliefs systems, he argues, have a childhood, an adolescense, and a maturity (represented by Kant). Except in his more speculative moments, Piaget clearly regards the structures that govern *perceptual* development, on the other hand, as invariants, biological givens, dictated by the necessities of species survival. For Piaget, as for Kant, the subject/object distinction is *the* epistemic norm. Indeed, one may read Piaget as describing (and universalizing) the "childhood" of *precisely* the Kantian knower, for whom the subjective unity of consciousness — the "I think" — is *the* central "moment" of knowing. To put this in a different way: One may read Kant as supplying a phenomenology of the very objectivity, now full-blown, that Piaget attempts to account for developmentally. For Piaget, as for Kant, that objectivity represents "the natural constitution of the human mind in relation to the world" (Hamlyn, 15). Although for Piaget, unlike Kant, it is part of a developmental process, it is nonetheless "the terminal stage" of that process, "inherent in the self-regulation of an equilibrated organism" (Furth, 18).

One may fault Piaget here, both for ethnocentrism and lack of consistency. His "developmental theory of ideas" describes the scientific and philosophic development, not of the human species, but of that particular intellectual arc that begins with the pre-Socratics and ends with the European "Enlightenment." The individual cognitive development that Piaget traces is also culturally located, derived as it is from studies of children who are growing up within modern Western norms of interaction between parent and child, child and environment. Even within Piaget's own framework, a more consistently relativist approach to perception and knowledge seems required. For, insofar as knowing is part of a biological structure, functional to the survival of the organism, and adaptive (in terms of the species) to the demands of the environment (all of which Piaget believes), then the possibility is opened up — theoretically, at least — of adaptive structures founded on radically different ways of encountering the world than those of the Kantian knower. The subject/object distinction itself may derive its survival value, and thus function as a dominant "epistemic norm," only within a certain environmental context (Piaget, 1971).

These ideas have application even if we remain within the Western European context. The historical nature of our prevailing construction of experience in terms of a self-conscious self confronting an external world of objects has been maintained explicitly by Julian Jaynes, Owen Barfield, and Morris Berman, and implicitly/accidentally by scholars such as C.S. Lewis. All of these writers emphasize fundamental differences between the dominant modes of experience of ancient and medieval cultures, and our modern norms of experience. Without going into their individual arguments, one can generalize the thrust of them: The subject/object distinction has, at the very least, *hardened* over time. On more extreme views, it is argued to be entirely absent from earlier cultures, cultures characterized by what Barfield has called "original participation."

> At some point between the lifetime of Homer and that of Plato, a sharp break occurred in Greek epistemology so as to turn it away from original participation . . . . It is difficult to conceive of a mentality that made virtually no distinction between subjective thought processes and what we call external phenomena, but it is likely that down to the time of the *Iliad* (ca. 900–850 B.C.) such was the case. The *Iliad* contains no words for internal states of mind . . . . The separation of mind and body, subject and object, is discernible as a historical trend by the sixth century before Christ; and the poetic, or Homeric mentality, in which the individual is immersed in a sea of contradictory experiences and learns about the world through emotional identification with it (original participation), is precisely what Socrates and Plato intended to destroy (Berman, 71).

The relevance of correspondences between individual development and historical development — such as those already presented and others to be presented later — is clear. At the very least, such correspondences open up the imagination to a consideration of the thoroughly *historical* character of our modern structuring of the relation between self and world. Looked at more specifically, they urge us to entertain the notion that the categories which we take for granted as experiential or theoretical "givens" — subjectivity, perspectivity, and, as I will propose in this and later essays, inwardness, locatedness, and objectivity (all "moments" of the subject/object distinction) — may be historical developments, or moments in the history of dominant (Western) norms of consciousness, each with its own birth, life, and decline. Once such lines of development have been imaginatively reconstructed, the insights of child psychology can also provide, as I will propose later, an illuminative framework for understanding some significant psychocultural changes that took place in the seventeenth century. In this and in the essay to follow, I focus on two such "givens" of modern experience — the innerness of thought and the locatedness of self in space and time — and attempt to explore the circumstances of their historical birth, that is, to attempt to put them, as Ortega says, in "status nascens."

In this essay, I will examine the Cartesian view of the mind as "inner arena." Looked at in cultural context, that view emerges, I will argue, as an aspect of what C.S. Lewis has called the "great process of internalization" that characterizes the transition from medieval to modern Western culture. In this essay, too, the argument begun in essay one, to "take Cartesian doubt seriously," is advanced still further: The "inner arena," I suggest, makes its first cultural appearance via the imagery of a distorting, untrustworthy inner space. "Innerness" makes its initial appearance, I argue, not (to borrow Rorty's image) as pristine "mirror of nature," but, in Bacon's words, as an obscuring "enchanted glass." Finally, I will turn once again to psychological theory for some developmental perspectives on the cultural birth of "innerness."

CULTURAL PERSPECTIVES ON THE "INVENTION OF THE MIND"

As Richard Rorty has brilliantly argued, the notion of mind as "inner arena" of ideas, standing between subject and world, is born in the Cartesian era (1979). However, this "invention," as Rorty calls it, needs to be understood as more than a move in a purely philosophical "conversation." Rather, the "new way with ideas" is the philosophical expression of a profound cultural development — of what Stephen Toulmin has called "the inwardness of mental life": the construction of experience as occuring deeply *within* and bounded by a self.

Philosophy, to be sure, contributed to this process. In Descartes, as Rorty points out, a crucial departure was made from the Aristotelian and medieval epistemologies: from the notion of "mind-as-reason" to the notion of "mind-as-consciousness" (p. 53). For Aristotle, there had been two modes of knowing, corresponding to the two ways that things may be known. On the one hand, there is *sensing*, which is the province of the body, and which is of the particular and material; on the other hand, there is *thought* (or reason), which is of the universal and immaterial. For Descartes, both these modes of knowing become subsumed under the category of *penser*, which embraces perceptions, images, ideas, pains, and volitions alike.

> What is a thing which thinks? It is a thing which doubts, understands, [conceives], affirms, denies, wills, refuses, which also imagines and feels (HR, I, 153).

The characteristic that unites all these states is that they are all *conscious* states.

> Thought is a word which covers everything that exists in us in such a way that we are immediately conscious of it. Thus all the operations of will, intellect, imagination, and of the senses are thoughts (HR, II, 52).

And "consciousness" was a new categorical umbrella which was at once to suggest the appropriateness of new imagery and metaphors. Whereas "Reason," for the Greeks and medievals, was a human faculty, resisting metaphors of locatedness, neither "inside" nor "outside" the human being,[3] "consciousness," for Descartes, was the quality of a certain sort of event — the sort of event distinguished from all other events precisely by being "located" in "inner space" rather than the external world.

The construction of thought as "inner" was to create new epistemological dilemmas, too. A new sort of mistake becomes possible: the judgment that what is "inside" — my modes of thought — "are similar or conformable to the things which are outside me" (HR, I, 160). Some ideas *may* be — and will turn out to be, for Descartes — "conformable" to external reality. But the "natural attitude" of assuming that they *all* are constitutes the "principal error ... we may meet with in them" (HR, I, 160).

With this stroke, the problem of "subjectivity" is born in philosophy. By "subjectivity" I mean the notion of influences proceeding from "within" the human being — not supplied by the world "outside" the perceiver — which are capable of affecting how the world is perceived. Although the "subjective" factor may be causally related to objects or events in the external world, it is related by way of elicitation, not by way of impression. Tastes, colors, odors, sounds, for Galileo, are "excited" by external objects but are not found "in them" (p. 276); the idea of the sun as very small, for Descartes, "proceeds from the sun" but does not resemble the sun (I, 161), and so on. "Subjectivity" is what stands, for Descartes and Galileo, between the knower and an accurate perception of the world. It is the barrier that casts the shadow of Cartesian anxiety, the possibility that our human capabilities may be such that we many never be able to reach the ordinary, changing world unless, as Dewey puts it, "the mind were protected against itself" (Dewey, 1957, p. 36). What it needs to be protected against is its own "subjectivity."

Consider the differences between the Greek and medieval view of the nature of error and the Cartesian view. The principal form that error takes, for Descartes, is in the judgment that the ideas that are in me "are similar or conformable to the things which are outside me." Even if we retain the imagery of "inner-outer" (which, as Rorty suggests, is inappropriate when talking of pre-Cartesian epistemology), such uncertainty about the capacity of the "inner" to lead to the "outer" is foreign to both Plato and Aristotle. Completely missing for the Greeks is the notion of an unreliable "inner space"; rather, there are two worlds (or, for Aristotle, it might be more correct to say two aspects of the same world) and two human faculties appropriate to each. Error is the result of confusion *between* two "outer" worlds — the sensible and the unchanging — not the result of misrepresentation of *the* outer world.

It is via the imagery of an untrustworthy "inner space" that the "mind" is born in the sixteenth and seventeenth centuries. It makes its initial appearance *not* as "mirror," the internal reflection of things "as they are," but as *subjectivity* — the capacity of the knower to bestow false inner projections on the outer world of things. What Descartes and Galileo here crystallized in philosophical form had already been anticipated in the work of Montaigne; the entire "inner arena" of the mind — that "erratic, dangerous and heedless tool" (in Frame, 233) — is capable of conferring its own "colors" on everything:

> Things in themselves may have their own weights and measures and qualities; but once inside, within us, she allots them their qualities as she sees fit. Death is frightful to Cicero, desirable to Cato, a matter of indifference to Socrates. Health, conscience, authority, knowledge, riches, beauty and their opposites — all are stripped on entry and receive from the soul new clothing, and the coloring that she chooses — brown, green, bright, dark, bitter, sweet, deep, superficial — and which each individual soul chooses; for they have not agreed together on their styles, rules and forms; each one is queen in her realm (in Frame, 135).

The birth of "subjectivity" had many cultural manifestations. In the sixteenth and seventeenth centuries we begin to see the old metaphysical dichotomy of change/permanence played out in an entirely new form. The new categories are not metaphysical but epistemological, and the new dichotomy is that of bias/neutrality. Since the "colors" that the mind bestows on objects vary from person to person, a "neutral" view of the object is impossible.

> ... who shall be fit to judge these differences? ... If he is old, he cannot judge the sense perception of old age, being himself a party in this dispute; if he is young, likewise; healthy, likewise; likewise sick, asleep, or awake. We would need someone exempt from all these qualities, so that with an unprejudiced judgment he might judge of these propositions as of things indifferent to him; and by that score we would need a judge that never was (Montaigne, in Frame, 247).

For the first time, the teachings of the past come to be seen not simply as mistaken or faulty but as capable of exerting a covert insidious influence *internally*, on "the mind." In the *Regulae*, Descartes speaks on the danger of being "infected" with the errors of the past (HR, I, 6); the chief problem is not that one's teachers were wrong or contradicted each other (although Descartes makes a point of this), but that they are one's *teachers*, and so capable of invisible influence (see also *Principles*, HR, I, 208; *Discourse*, HR, I, 88). The theme, once again, was anticipated by Montaigne.

> Our mind moves only on faith, being bound and constrained to the whim of others' fancies, a slave and a captive under the authority of their teaching. We have been so well accustomed to leading strings that we have no free motion left; our rigor and liberty are extinct (in Frame, 35).

When Aristotle criticizes Plato, there is none of this concern over the consequences, *within the pupil*, of having been a student. The sense is, rather, that the natural order of development is to have been apprenticed, to have seen the mistakes of one's teachers, and to have corrected them. It is only in the sixteenth century that a theme which is to become so prominent in the modern era begins to emerge; the theme is the notion that the human being — especially the human mind — may be the helpless "product" of the past, brought to its present state by a causal chain of historical events and parental influences (and, later, economic or material factors, unconscious events, social "conditioning," etc.) over which it has no control and of which it may be in deepest ignorance.

Although originally associated with the influence of the organs of sense, the notion of a vulnerable and untrustworthy "inner space," once established as an image, became the model of the mind itself. And the indictment of the naked senses contributed to this in a way which went beyond the obvious result of casting sense experience itself into suspicion. For, although sense experience was previously conceptualized as a body capacity (Rorty, 51–52), colors, odors, tastes, and so forth, were not therefore "in us." Now, as firmly located "in us," there is reason to wonder what more that we believed to issue from "out there" may be discovered to have only an inner, "subjective" reality.

The concern with "subjectivity" is part of what C. S. Lewis calls "the great process of internalization" that characterizes the transition from medieval to modern culture (p. 215). That process turned "genius" from a visiting spirit into a personal quality of mind. It transformed the idea of "authority" into the notion of inner "influence." And it created a new sense of experience as deeply *within* and bounded by a self. According to many scholars of the era, such a sense was not prominent in the medieval experience of the world.

> When we think casually, we think of consciousness as situated at some point in space . . . even those who achieve the intellectual contortionism of denying that there is such a thing as consciousness, feel that this denial comes from inside their own skins . . . . This was not the background picture before the scientific revolution. The background picture then was of man as a microcosm within the macrocosm. It is clear that he did not feel himself isolated by his skin from the world outside to quite the same extent that we do. He was integrated or mortised into it, each different part of him being united to a different part of it by some invisible thread. In his relation to his environment, the man of the middle ages was rather less like an island, rather more like an embryo (Barfield, 78) . . . .

Morris Berman agrees with Barfield that a "participating consciousness" — which is structured around a merger with nature rather than detachment from nature — was still alive in the pre-Renaissance experience of the world (although it had been steadily undermined and attenuated, according to Berman, from the time of Plato). He finds it, for example, in the "common denominators" of medieval consciousness (whether Aristotelian or hermetic) — the doctrines of *resemblance, sympathy,* and *antipathy,* which connect *all* domains of the universe through a network of shared meanings (pp. 69–75). More specifically, the alchemical and magical traditions — the "hermetic wisdom" — are viewed, by Berman, as the dying gasp of participation as a genuine mode of *knowledge,* "dedicated to the notion that real knowledge occurred only via the union of subject and object, in a psychic-emotional identification with images rather than a purely intellectual examination of concepts" (p. 73).

During the Renaissance, as Claudio Guillen argues, European culture became "interiorized" (pp. 306–310). It is in art and literature that the change is most dramatically expressed. For the medievals and early Renaissance, there is no radical disjunction between the "inner" reality and outward appearance, but rather "a close relation between the movement of the body and movement of the soul" (Baxandall, 60). In drama, facial and postural gestures were regarded as transparently expressive of intentions and thoughts of the speaker (Guillen, 307). Dance was regarded as "an action demonstrative of spiritual movement" in which, as Alberti says, "the movements of the soul are recognized in the movements of the body" (Baxandall, 60). And the "most important thing" for the painter to learn, according to Leonardo, "are the movements proper to the mental condition of each living being" (Baxandall, 60). Michael Baxandall, in *Painting and Experience in Fifteenth Century Italy*, even suggests that a conventional lexicon of gestures was employed in the creation and interpretation of artworks, much like the code of gestures (for disgust, joy, irony, etc.) in the Italian "guidebooks" for preachers (p. 64).

Gradually, a decisive change begins to occur. The portrayal of the "inner life" — both as a dramatic problem (how can the playwright depict the experience of the character?) and as a subject of literary exploration — becomes an issue. In Shakespeare, a new theme emerges: the "hidden substance" of the self — the notion that the experience of individuals is fundamentally opaque, even inaccessible to others, who can only take the "outer view" on it. Hamlet here gives voice to the experience of sharp distinction between outer, public self and the "interiority" of the subjective life:

> Seems, madam, nay it is; I know not "seems."
> 'Tis not alone my inky cloak, good mother,
> Nor customary suits of solemn black,
> Nor windy suspiration of forced breath,
> No, nor the fruitful river in the eye,
> Nor the dejected havior of the visage,
> Together with all forms, moods, shapes of grief,
> That can denote me truly; these indeed seem,
> For they are actions that a man might play,
> But I have that within which passes show;
> These but the trappings and the suits of woe.
> (I. II, 76–86)

The "inner life" becomes, too, an object of voluptuous and unrestrained introspection. Montaigne, once again, is a striking example.

I turn my gaze inward, I fix it there and keep it busy . . . I look inside myself; I continually observe myself, I take stock in myself, I taste myself . . . I roll about in myself (in Frame, 273).

"Myself" here is neither the public self, a social or familial identity, or even the voice of personal conscience, belief or commitment. It is an experiential "space inside," deeply interior, and at the same time capable of objectification and examination.

The *Meditations* — in its form and in its content — is the most compelling example we have of a thoroughgoing confrontation with the "inwardness of mental life." Augustine's *Confessions* embody a stream of consciousness, to be sure, but they very rarely — e.g., in some of the passages on time — confront that stream as an *object* of exploration. Descartes provides the first real "phenomenology" of the mind, and one of the central results of that phenomenology is the disclosure of the deep epistemological alienation that attends the sense of mental interiority: the enormous gulf that must separate what is conceived as occurring "in here" from that which, correspondingly, must lay "out there."[4] The central inquiry of Meditation II, and the first formulation of what was to become *the* epistemological question for philosophers until Kant, is "whether any of the object of which I have ideas *within me* exist *outside of me*." (HR, I, 161; emphasis added.) Under such circumstances, *cogito ergo sum* is, indeed, the only emphatic reality, for to be assured of its truth, we require nothing but confrontation with the inner stream itself. Beyond the direct and indubitable "I am," the meditation on the self can lead to no other truths without God to bridge the gulf between the "inner" and the "outer."

DEVELOPMENTAL PERSPECTIVES ON THE "INVENTION OF THE MIND"

In the preceding section, I have discussed the construction of thought as "inner" (and the correlative construction of world as "outer" or "external") as an historical emergence. Turning now to developmental theory, we can see some provocative correspondences. For the human child, the distinction between "inner" and "outer," as we have learned from Piaget, is gradually acquired. At first, the child's experience is of absolute continuity between self and world (she/he is "mortised into it," to borrow Barfield's evocative phrase). There is neither an experience of *external* reality nor an experience of *internal* reality. They are one and the same. Slowly, through a process of exploration and interaction with the world (in early infancy, the mother,) in which the child's boundaries are tested and limits are established, subjectivity becomes ever more internally aware, and the object-world becomes ever more external and autonomous. The terminus of this course of cognitive development (whose emotional dimensions will be explored later) is the adult "norm" of experiencing oneself as "both fully 'in' and at the same time basically separate from the world out there" (Mahler, 333).

Such developmental perspectives may be thought to be unique to contemporary conceptions of the self. But strikingly and surprisingly, *Descartes* proposes some developmental insights in a similar vein. As characterized by him, childhood is, first and foremost, a period of *egocentrism* (clearly in the Piagetian sense): the complete inability to distinguish between subject and object. Descartes's explanation for this is that in infancy the mind, "newly united" to the body, is "swamped" (B, 8) and "immersed" within it (HR, I, 237), "wholly occupied in perceiving and feeling the ideas of pain, pleasure, heat, cold and other similar ideas which arise from its union and intermingling with the body" (PL, 111; see also B, 8). As body, according to Descartes, we are completely reactive and nondiscriminative. Because the body is after all, *res extensa*, a network of automatic responses to the environment around it and processes occuring within it, as infants "swamped" by the body we are unable to make the most basic distinctions — e.g., between an inner occurence and an external event. One might say, in fact, that the distinction has no meaning for the body.

It is the child's "immersion" in the body, and the egocentrism that results from this immersion, that is responsible for "childhood prejudices" which later persist in the form of adult philosophical confusion between primary and secondary qualities, the "preconceptions of the senses" and the dictates of reason, and so on. As children, we knew much sufficiently clearly (i.e., with great impact and intensity) but "nothing distinctly" (HR, I, 237). We judged

> that there was more or less reality in each body, according as the impressions made on body were more or less strong. Hence came the belief that there was much more substance or corporeal reality in rocks or metals than in air or water, because the sensations of hardness and weight were much more strongly felt. And thus it was that air was only regarded as anything when it was agitated by some wind, and we experienced it to be either hot or cold . . . . And because the stars did not give more light than tiny lighted candles, we did not hold them to be larger than such flames . . . . And we have in this way been imbued with a thousand other such prejudices from infancy, which in later youth we quite forgot we had accepted without sufficient examination, admitting them as though they were of perfect truth and certainty . . . . (*Principles*, HR, I, 250)

Descartes here quite accurately apprehends what Piaget describes as the developing child's tendency to see objects in terms of "subjective groupings": as partially constituted by the child's actions, feelings, position, and so forth, rather than by their own objective aspects (1954, p. 168). He is also, of course, quite consciously invoking the categories (substance, corporeal reality, etc.) of the philosophical traditions that preceded him — criticism of those traditions is a constant subtext (and often an explicit text) in Descartes's writings. By invoking these traditional metaphysical categories, Descartes can be read as implying that this predecessors' systems of thought have not advanced much past the condition of infancy. This is not to say that Descartes is charging his philosophical forefathers with actually experiencing the world as infants do. Rather, his claim is that underlying their extremely sophisticated formulations are the epistemological residua of infancy, implicitly accepted and systematized into philosophical dogma.

Descartes's developmental thinking is nascent and fragmentary. He belongs to an era for which the very concept of the self which is the focus of developmental theory is still newborn and fragile. Indeed, it is just this newness and fragility, I propose, that underlie the Cartesian sense, discussed in essay one, of the tenuousness and discontinuous nature of both inner life and external world, and the deep Cartesian anxiety over the chasm between self and world. If we imagine the distinction between self and world as *in some sense* newly constructed (this sense will be further specified in the next essay), we can also imagine both that the boundaries of each are still blurry, *and* at the same time that the distance between them must be experienced as profound. We can imagine, in turn, that the emotional consequences of this new epistemological experience of distance and alienation between self and world must have been significant.

Once again, the categories of developmental theory provide a tool for exploring this emotional dimension. In becoming a separate self, in the disentangling of self from primary union with the mother, the child is not only learning how to be an "epistemic subject" (according to our modern norms, at any rate); the child is also learning to live in the absence of the sense of continual nurture and intimacy, of absolute emotional union with the mother, that characterizes womb-life and the earliest stages of infancy. This process of emotional separation from the mother is probably the most wrenching tear in the fabric of human connection that we ever experience. Every major step in the direction of individuation, according to the psychologist Margaret Mahler, revives our "eternal longing" for the "ideal state of self" in which mother and child were one, and recognition of our ever-increasing distance from it. "Side by side with the growth of his emotional life, there is a noticeable waning ... of his [previous] relative obliviousness to the mother's presence. Increased separation anxiety can be observed ... a seemingly constant concern with the mother's whereabouts" (p. 337). Although we become more or less reconciled to our separateness, the process of individuation and its anxieties "reverberates throughout the life cycle. It is never finished, it can always be reactivated" (p. 333).

May not such a process "reverberate," too, on the cultural level? Perhaps some cultural eras *compensate* for the pain of personal individuation better than others, through a mother imagery of the cosmos (such as was dominant, throughout the Chaucerian and Elizabethan eras) that assuages the anxiety of our actual separateness as individuals. On the other hand, during periods in which long-established images of symbiosis and cosmic unity *break down* (as they did during the period of the "scientific revolution"), may we not expect an increase in self-consciousness, and anxiety over the distance between self and world — a constant concern, to paraphrase Mahler, over the "whereabouts of the world?" All these, as I have suggested, are central motifs in the *Meditations*.

Reunion with the (mother) world is, however, impossible for Descartes and for the Cartesian era. Medieval "participating consciousness," for which the categories of inner and outer, self and world, human and natural, were not rigorously opposed, had ceased to provide viable models of knowledge for the more aggressive, progress-oriented science and technology of the seventeenth century. New models of knowledge had yet to replace them. It is in this gap that Cartesian anxiety wells up.

It is striking that only God the father can provide the reassurance Descartes needs. In the absence of a sense of connectedness with the natural world — and that includes, for Descartes, a sense of connectedness with one's own body — only a guarantee "from above" can alleviate epistemological anxiety. The change may also be described in terms of separation from the *maternal* — the immanent realms of earth, nature, the authority of the body — and a compensatory turning toward the *paternal* for legitimation through external regulation, transcendent values, and the authority of law. On the basis of a psychoanalytic exploration of these themes, Karl Stern proposes that Cartesian absolutism was deeply psychologically motivated by Descartes's early maternal deprivation, indeed, was a reaction-formation to that deprivation. My own approach, in the final essay of this study, will be to examine such ideas on the level of *cultural* rather than individual psychology. To set the stage for this analysis, I now turn to the task of explicating the provocative notions upon which my analysis depends — namely, the notions of cultural "separation," "individuation," and "maternal deprivation."

Chapter Four

INDIVIDUATION AND LOCATEDNESS: A CULTURAL DRAMA OF PARTURITION

> *When I consider the brief span of my life absorbed into an eternity which comes*
> *before and after . . . the small space I occupy and which I see swallowed up in the infinite*
> *immensity of spaces of which I know nothing and which know nothing of me, I take*
> *fright and am amazed to see myself here rather than there: there is no reason for me to*
> *be here rather than there, now rather than then. Who puts me here? By whose command*
> *and act were this time and place allotted to me?*
>
> (Pascal, *Pensées*)

Among the images employed by writers in discussing the transition from the Middle Ages to the early modern period, metaphors from birth and infancy are prominent. "The world did in her Cradle take a fall," mourned Donne in the *Anatomy of the World* (1611), grieving for a lost world as well as for Elizabeth Drury. Ortega y Gasset describes the "human drama which began in 1400 and ends in 1650" as a "drama of parturition" (p. 184). Arthur Koestler compares the finite universe to a "nursery" and, later, to a womb: "Homo sapiens had dwelt in a universe enveloped by divinity as by a womb; now he was being expelled from the womb" (p. 218). Owen Barfield, as we have seen, speaks of the medieval as an "embryo." Such imagery may be more appropriate than any of these authors intended. As individuals, according to Margaret Mahler, our true psychological birth comes when we begin to experience our separateness from the mother, when we begin to *individuate* from her. Substituting "world" for "mother" (and, as will be discussed later, the world of the Renaissance and Middle Ages *was* a mother-world, symbolically, imagistically, and, perhaps, experientially), such a process of individuation *did* occur in the sixteenth and seventeenth centuries. Or at least, the art, literature, and philosophy of the era tell such a story.

So far, I have approached this story of individuation through the era's emerging sense of (and preoccupation with) the "inwardness of mental life": the structuring of experience as *interior* and enclosed within a self. Correlative to such an experience of self/innerness is the experience of the world as decisively *external*, as *not-self*. And for Descartes, as we have seen, an epistemological chasm indeed separates a highly self-conscious self from a universe that now lies "out there." Dominant motifs in the earlier *Meditations* are a heightened and pervasive experience of self as inwardness ("I think, therefore I am") and anxiety over that self's connection with "outer" reality.

Such anxiety is peculiarly modern. The medievals *had* no "problem of knowledge" (at least, not as we conceive it, in terms of certifying a correspondence between ideas and external world). Nor was the self/world dichotomy a characteristic way of talking about the universe. Rather, as Carolyn Merchant has argued (1980), the dominating ontological metaphor was of the universe as a single "organism," whose domains (although hierarchically ordered) were characterized by interdependence and interconnection rather than mutual exclusivity. According to Owen Barfield and others, this was not simply a philosophical or ideological superstructure but a mode of experiencing being human and being-in-the-world that permeated ordinary language, and even the most basic levels of perception. The human being of the Middle Ages, Barfield argues, perceived itself in continuity with the rest of the universe, in a way that we can no longer precisely duplicate, and can only imagine.

Certainly, if we turn to consider medieval art, we are forced to entertain the possibility that in that art is represented a very different perceptual world from the Euclidean world we are used to. What is distinctive about medieval art is the absence of *perspective* — that is, the absence of an (imaginary) fixed observer, located at a particular point in space, from whose "point of view" the scene is presented. Perhaps this says less about medieval perception than about the history of artistic conventions. But Owen Barfield insists that the reason why perspective was not discovered before the Renaissance[1] was because it did not represent the medieval experience of the world.

> Before the scientific revolution the world was more like a garment men wore about them than a stage on which they moved. In such a world the convention of perspective was unnecessary .... It was as if the observers were themselves in the picture. Compared with us they felt themselves and the objects around them and the words that expressed those objects, immersed together in something like a clear lake of — what shall we say? — of "meaning," if you choose (p. 94–5).

By extreme contrast, consider Pascal's despair at what seems to him an arbitrary and impersonal "allotment" in "the infinite immensity of spaces of which I know nothing and which knows nothing of me . . . There is no reason for me to be here rather than there, now rather than then. Who put me here?" The sense of personal boundedness and *locatedness*, of "me-here-now" (and *only* "here-now") is acute. Its association with a loss of "meaning" is undeniable. Is it too soon to speak here of cultural "separation anxiety"? Whatever one wishes to call it, a similar anxiety, as I have suggested, is at the heart of Descartes's need for a God to sustain both his existence and his inner life from moment to moment, to provide a reassurance of permanence and connection between self and world. Once, such connection had not been a question.

Let us examine in more detail some of the issues raised here. I begin with a "clue": some striking similarities between the "pictorial space" of medieval art and the actual "perceptual space" of children, as described by Jean Piaget. I want to stress, however, that in presenting these correspondences, I do not mean to suggest that medievals saw the world as children do at a certain stage in their development. The perceptual egocentrism of the child can only be supported, in terms of survival, by a totally dependent being. Moreover, neither art nor literature, neither language nor conceptual intelligence is possible for a totally egocentric being, who has to learn to "objectify" the world perceptually before it can begin to *represent* it in any way to itself or to others.

These correspondences, rather, are signposts and guides to the interpretation of the "text" of medieval culture; they suggest a way of *reading* some of the elements of that culture that appear most mysterious and alien to us. They lead us to entertain the question that perhaps this was a culture for which the basic perceptual separation of subject and world, although accomplished, played a far less formidable role in the total experience of the human being.

We are all familiar with states (religious, erotic, creative, aesthetic, parental, or empathic, for example) in which the sense of separateness, from others or from the world, remains intact on one level (in that we do not perceive the world, as the infant does, as a sheer undifferentiated continuum), yet obliterated on another. Such states may seem emotionally discontinuous with ordinary experience. But might that not be at least in part a measure of how highly developed our "normal" sense of personal boundedness has become? Alternatively, can we not conceive of a culture within which the sense of continuity between self and the world, self and others, is a more prominent feature of *ordinary* experience, one in which such a sense at least shares the stage with the perceptual organization of self and objects in space and time? In the next section of this essay, I will explore this possibility, surveying the work of a number of authors who have argued for the historical nature of perception, presenting evidence that our own perspectival norms of perception, which presuppose the dominance of a sense of "psychic distance" between subject and world, are a cultural product. Such a sense of psychic distance is related to what I consider to be a key difference between the experiential world of modernity and the world that preceded it, namely, the emergence of the sense of the locatedness, or situatedness, of self in space and time. The emergence of such a sense of locatedness, and the consequent generation of certain characteristically modern anxieties, consitute what I am here calling "a drama of parturition."

PERCEPTUAL WORLDS

The perceptual organization of self and objects in space and time is, according to Piaget, a developmental accomplishment which the child reaches only after having passed through earlier stages of perceptual development. At the earliest stage, there are neither external objects — which for Piaget, as for Kant, in order to *be* objects, must be connected in an intelligible way within the totality of a spatio-temporal network — nor is there an internal world, conscious of itself as located within that network and related spatially to other objects within it. At this stage, the spatial world is a universe of "presentations," whose images are endowed with emotional, kinesthetic, and sensori-motor qualities as well as physical ones (1954, p. 240), and within which the personal actions of the child and changes in things are not perceptually distinguished. Changes in the states of objects are perceived as extensions of the child's activity, or, to put the same thing in another way, the child is "absorbed in things" (1954, p. 116). The most general formulation for all this is that the child lacks a perception of space as the framework of the universe, in which self and objects are *located* and related to each other. There is no "perspective" on things, because to *have* a perspective it is necessary to have a sense of personal locatedness — which in turn presupposes the experience of a distinguishable self and a world lying outside the self. For the very young child, such "psychic distance" on the world is absent.

So too for medieval art. It seems clear that for the medieval aesthetic imagination, *absorption* in the world rather than *locatedness* in the world was central. It is the latter mode of experience — of the self as discretely located in space and geometrically related to other objects so located — that the perspective painting tries to recreate on the "illusionist" space of the canvas, through the adoption of the "fiction" of the fixed observer and the plotting out of the objects to be represented as more or less remote from that observer. This, of course, had become the dominant artistic convention by the seventeenth century. But in medieval art, *nothing* is spatially "fixed." Sizes of objects were determined, not by plotting their spatial relations to each other and to the viewer, but according to each object's place in a hierarchy of power, strength, or importance.[2] Often, the same figure would appear several times, the purpose being "to represent all possible relationships that affected him . . . by a simultaneous description of various actions" (McLuhan, 127). The effect is baffling to a modern viewer, who expects realistic paintings to depict the nexus of spatial relations surrounding the figure. In medieval art, attention to individual detail rather than spatial unity of conception was foremost (Huizinga, 278; Edgerton, 21).

Most strikingly, the "fiction" of the fixed beholder is entirely absent. Instead, the spectator, as the art historian Samuel Edgerton describes it, is "invited" to become "absorbed within the visual world . . . to walk about, experiencing structures, almost tactiley, from many different sides, rather than from a single, overall vantage" (p. 9). This "sensori-motor" participation of the subject is actually part of the constitution of the represented *object*, much as the developing child's own motor activity, as a perception of independent objects is gradually being formed, partially constitutes the perceived object. At this stage in the child's development, things are seen in terms of "subjective groupings," that is, the objective world "changes" with the position and movement of the child. So too we find, in medieval art, the common phenomenon of "split representation," which presents objects, not as they would appear relative to each other and with respect to position and distance from a fixed observer, but as they might appear to a mobile subject, touching, exploring, and considering the object from all angles. This mobility of the subject is portrayed in the object itself, by showing more sides than would be seen "in (fixed) perspective."

Most striking to a modern viewer, of course, is the absence of such "perspective." This is the chief reason why medieval canvases appear to us as spatially incoherent, distorted, and without a center of orientation. We are accustomed to perspectival representation — at least, we expect it from pictures that make a claim to "realism." But at the time of Brunelleschi's famous first demonstration of the application of the principles of perspective to painting (1425), the result was experienced as magical and incredible by those who witnessed the demonstration. And indeed, artists would sometimes use a mirror to demonstrate to their audiences just how magical their effects were; the mirror provided the "real-life" framed perspective image that the painting could be seen to duplicate.

The fact that *we* no longer experience perspective paintings as magical illusions could signify merely that we are used to the convention in art. But could it not also signify our embodied acculturation to a mode of geometrical *seeing* uncharacteristic of the dominant perceptual modes of previous cultures? The perspective painting, after all, is also *unlike* reality in many ways: "There are many more right angles, many more straight lines and many more regular solids in Quattrocento paintings than there are in nature or had been in earlier paintings" (Baxandall, 127). Artists often had to employ cumbersome artificial means to achieve the "fiction" of the fixed observer, Albrecht Dürer proposing the device of a glass plate between painter and subject, and a chin rest to keep the painter's head from moving. Artists required aids to help them to portray objects in "correct" spatial proportion, as well; Alberti recommended a specially woven veil — called an "intersection" — which when worn over the painter's eyes, "divided" the visual field into square sections, and enabled the artist to "put everything in its right place" on panels or walls divided similarly (Alberti, 69).

The "point of view" of the perspective painting, moreover, spatially freezes perception, isolating one "moment" from what is normally experienced as part of a visual continuum. The perceptual psychologist James Gibson provides a distinction that is useful here: that between the "visual world" and the "visual field." The visual *world* is "the familiar, ordinary scene of daily life," the way things appear to us as we go about our business: moving, touching, doing, and paying little attention to the process of perception itself. Within this world vision is interrelated with all the other senses, and with cognitive knowledge: "Solid objects look solid, square objects look square, horizontal objects look horizontal, and the book lying across the room looks as big as the book lying in front of you" (p. 26). The visual *field* is what we perceive when we fixate with our eyes and pay attention to what lies within the frozen boundaries of our vision: when we make a "picture" of the scene before us.

The visual world is stable — and its stability is a function of its continuousness: Objects retain a constancy despite changes in the viewer's position. The moment we attempt to "freeze" perception (e.g., by fixing on a succession of distinct visual fields), its stability falls apart. We encounter not a world, but a series of framed images, each one different from the other, each one a particular "perspective." We become aware "of how things change in shape, size, and proportion with respect to position and distance from the fixed eyes (and from each other)" (Edgerton, 10). It is only in the visual field, too, that the central fact of linear perspective — the progressive convergence of parallel lines as they recede in the distance — becomes prominent (Gibson, p. 35)[3] and that visual scenes divide neatly into figures and background (Gibson, 39).

"Pictorial seeing," Gibson concludes, "differs astonishingly from ordinary seeing" (p. 42). Merleau-Ponty subtly and evocatively describes this difference as it appears to him:

> In spontaneous vision . . . at every moment I was swimming in the world of things and overrun by a horizon of things to see which could not possibly be seen simultaneously with what I was seeing but *by this very fact* were simultaneous with it . . . my glance, running freely over depth, height, and width, was not subordinated to any point of view, because it adopted and rejected each one in turn . . . . I had the experience of a world of teeming, exclusive things which could be embraced only by means of a temporal cycle in which each gain is simultaneously a loss. [In perspective], this world crystallizes into an ordered perspective within which backgrounds resign themselves to being merely backgrounds, inaccessible and vague as required, where objects in the foreground lose something of their aggressiveness, order their interior lines according to the common law of the spectacle, already preparing to become backgrounds when necessary, and where finally nothing looks into one's vision and adopts the figure of being present. The whole scene is in the past, in the mode of completion and eternity. Everything adopts an air of propriety and discretion. Things no longer call upon me and I am not compromised by them (pp. 52–3).

The spatial organization of *medieval* art seems designed to represent "spontaneous vision," to convey the sense, which Merleau-Ponty describes above, of "swimming" in a world of "teeming, exclusive things." In terms of Gibson's distinction between the visual world and the visual field, medieval paintings represent the visual *world*; they capture the experience of walking about, orienting oneself to objects from all sides, "cognizant of their complete form" even when not actually "seen" (Edgerton, 10). The common medieval artistic phenomenon of "split representation" (the "representation of three-dimensional objects as if split apart and pressed flat, so that the picture shows more sides and parts of the object than could be seen from a single viewpoint" [Edgerton, 14]) is "impossible" only from the point of view of the frozen visual *field* — the point of view of "completion" and "propriety." From the point of view of the visual field, too, painting the same person or object twice in the same spatial field is an incoherency. But from the point of view of the visual *world*, the variety of a person's (or object's) relations to other persons and objects is part of what composes the object's identity. The "complete form" of the object includes the nonvisual knowledge we have of the object: The human actions associated with the object, its human "meanings," coalesce with the information provided by the senses to form the stability and value of the object. "Things call upon us," in Merleau-Ponty's terms.

The examination of medieval art prompts us to entertain the possibility that the medieval perceptual world may have been one within which the visual world was far more prominent than in ours. And perhaps the purely visual aspect of perception was not nearly so dominant, and thus not nearly so capable of insisting on its laws as the standard of coherence for a painting.[4] Marshall McLuhan, for example, has argued that it is only by means of the intense isolation of the visual senses from the other senses — a process which occurs only in "print cultures" — that real facility at perspectival seeing develops. The ability to "discover reality" in the perspective painting requires visual skills — the ability to adopt a detached point of view and to scan a static frame — that are developed, McLuhan argues, only through experience at silent, private reading of the printed page (p. 43). Some African cultures, for example, have not developed the "psychic distance" required to interpret perspectival representations.

That perception has a human history is a central theme, too, in the work of Patrick Heelan. Our dominant Euclidean norms of perception, he argues, are themselves "a product of scientific culture and an artifact of a technologically reconstructed human environment" (p. 1). That environment is full of architectural and cultural "cues" that teach us to "read" the world Euclideanly and to classify as "illusion" anything that clashes with our expectations of the "text."

The cues that Heelan has in mind are in the "carpentry" of our surroundings: "simple engineered forms of fixed markers, like buildings, equally spaced lamp posts and roads of constant width . . . mobile markers, like automobiles, trains" (p. 251). Such works of engineering act as cues in the sense that "from their paradigmatic Euclidean geometrical forms is 'read' the fact that things of different sizes or in different locations can be similar, a property characteristic of Euclidean space . . . " (p. 251).

Such carpentry was not much in evidence in the Renaissance, of course, but it was on the rise. Edgerton considers it significant enough to point, for example, to the "increasing geometrization of the land" resulting from the growth of centralized land management: "The carefully striated terraces . . . the parallel strings of grape vines" (p. 35), he claims, impressed Alberti.

The sensibilities that would find the geometrization of the environment congenial were on the rise as well. The new social importance of commerce and banking, and the increasing sophistication of bookkeeping, produced a class of merchants, Edgerton suggests, "more and more disposed to a visual world that would accord with the tidy principles of mathematical order that they applied to their bank ledgers" (p. 39). And traditions in middle class education were developing, in which arithmetic and geometry were prominent, as well as the skills of land surveying and engineering. It is in such schools that Brunelleschi and other early perspective painters received their training.

"It is necessary for the painter to learn geometry" (p. 90), Alberti unequivocally declared. It was necessary, too, for the Renaissance merchant. Since barrels, sacks, and bales did not come in standardized sizes, it was essential to be able to calculate, or "gauge," the volume of a container. Increasing trade had pressed the need for methods of dealing with the problem of currency exchange: Every merchant had to know how to apply the "rule of three," a standard method of determining proportions. It was used, too, by the Renaissance painter in determining, for example, body proportions (Baxandall, 96).

The similarities in training between the perspective painters and their prospective public — the commercial class — resulted, Baxandall argues, in a common "cognitive style" (p. 91) which both informed the paintings and rendered them accessible to the viewer. "To the commercial man almost anything was reducible to geometrical figures underlying any surface irregularities," a habit "very close to the painter's analysis of appearance" (p. 90). And the painters themselves would often include stock objects used in gauging exercises — cisterns, columns, brick towers, paved floors, pavilions — in their paintings (p. 87), as if to provide the cues that would facilitate the viewer's "reading" of the text of the painting.

A great many factors, therefore, have contributed to our acculturation to geometrical seeing. It would be as misleading to say that perspective paintings "taught us" to see geometrically as it would be to conclude that the convention of perspective was the first form of artistic representation to portray the world as it always "really" was seen. The earliest perspective painters were already highly influenced by a developing geometric and mathematical sensibility in the culture around them. On the other hand, it is only *after* the conventionalization of linear perspective in art — and, according to Karsten Harries and others, largely as a result of *its* influence — that the homogeneous, infinite space "implied" in the perspective painting becomes the "official" space of the culture:[5] Brunelleschi's demonstration occurred one hundred years before "infinity opened its jaws" with Copernicus's denial of the rotation of the heavens around the earth. And it was not until Giordano Bruno (1584) that the positive assertion of an infinite universe was unequivocally made (Koyré, 39; Lovejoy, 108). Yet pictorial perspectivity seems to require the conception of a uniform, infinite space transcending objects and uniting them geometrically: "Kepler's postulation, in . . . 1604, that parallel lines meet at a point in infinity was the independent mathematical recognition of an operational fact implicit in Alberti's construction and indirectly stated by him in his text" (Ivins, 10). Infinity seems to have "opened its jaws" for the perspective painter before the scientist.

LOCATEDNESS

There is obviously a complicated dialectic at work in such fundamental historical changes in the conception and perception of the universe. I do not pretend to be able to sort out the lines of causality and interaction. But what is clear is that at some point the "illusionist space" of the perspective painting and the "theoretic space" of the culture became fully *congruent*. According to Panofsky, such congruence is a state of affairs toward which every historical period strives, seeking its own aesthetic "answer" to the problem of representing space, correlating intuitively to the intellectual conception of space dominant or in the ascendency in that period.[6]

Just as post-Copernican theoretic space and the aesthetic space of the perspective painting are perfectly matched, so were medieval conceptions of space and medieval conventions of representation. The medievals, like the Greeks, "experienced the spatial," as Heidegger says, "on the basis not of extension, but . . . as *chora*, which signifies . . . that which is occupied by what stands there" (Heidegger, 54). So Plato's image, in the *Timeaus*, is of *chora* as a "receptacle."[7] And for Aristotle, space is "the boundary of the containing body at which it is in contact with the contained body" (*Physics* 212a5), separating objects rather than underlying them and informing us about the distances between them. For Aristotle, space *contains*; it does not *locate*.

Correspondingly, for the medieval aesthetic imagination, locatedness was not a central category. Space and time were not as important in establishing relations between things as were eternal meanings, logical connections, and spiritual affinities (Burtt, 27; Lewis, 94; Huizinga, 201–227; Barfield, 94–95). The world was "a place of interconnected *meanings*, not objects" (Huizinga, 201), in which the conventions of language and art therefore stressed the symbolic continuities between physical events and spiritual aspirations rather than the spatial and temporal relations between individual things. Medieval painting, as we have seen, embodies this ontology, within which even space itself, according to Barfield, was "humanized."

> . . . the celestial revolutions . . . were approached in a way that suggests that what we call space was conceived rather as a kind of unindividuated, all-enclosing continuum, or mental mobile, for which perhaps *wisdom* is the best modern word we can find. Space, as a mindless, wisdomless, lifeless void, was not a common notion . . . it is only when space itself has become . . . simply the absence of phenomena, conceived in the phenomenal mode, that perspective takes the place of participation (pp. 148–149).

The medieval *aesthetic* imagination, then, shares with the perceptual world of the developing child the correlative structure of a not yet fully "de-subjectified" world and a not yet fully "objectified" self — a self which does not primarily experience itself as "located," along with the other objects of the world, within space and time. Subject and object are united through shared *meanings*, rather than rendered ontologically separate.

In the sixteenth and seventeenth centuries, on the other hand, *locatedness* emerges as a central category of thought. We have already seen how the inescapable locatedness of *ideas* in (cultural) space and time begins to haunt writers of the period. Strikingly, the epistemological implications of this — the possibility that there may be no neutral, unbiased, "Archimedean" view of things — begins, in the seventeenth century, to be couched via the cognitive metaphors of "perspective" and "point of view." "All we can set our eyes upon is these intricate mazes of life," writes William Drummond of Hawthornden, "is but Alchemy, vain perspective and deceiving shadows, appearing far other ways afar off, than when looked upon at a near distance" (Guillen, 301). And Pascal: "In painting, the rules of perspective decide the right place, but how will it be decided when it comes to truth and morality" (p. 35)?[8]

The historical era, too, becomes — for the first time — a *locating* category. The historians Myron Gilmore and Lucien Febvre argue that the sense of the historical era as particular context — what Gilmore calls the "historical imagination" — was born in the Renaissance. Gilmore points, as evidence of this, to the lack of a concept of "anachronism" in the Middle Ages. The notion of anachronism — which renders it odd, for us, to see medieval art in which ancient gods and goddesses are dressed in medieval garb, or Christian saints in Greek attire[9] — depends, argues Gilmore, on the sense of "historical distance," of the differences which separate one era from another. The Middle Ages, on the contrary, understood human history as a unified story, a single spectacle of events extending from creation to the Last Judgement (Gilmore, 79). The items of importance were the continuities, not the differences.

Another example of the new Renaissance understanding of context and period is the artistic and literary interest in anecdote, local color, and historical setting — the "individuating detail" — rather than "eternal images belonging to all times and places" (Febvre, 52). Not only costumes become specific to era, but setting: Instead of occurring within a "vague world of faith and hope," as previous representations had, in the fifteenth-century St. Christopher in the Brussels Museum, claims Febvre, "we can tell where and almost in what year the scene is set" (p. 53).

A final illustration of the development of the concept of historical "locatedness" is the new cultural prominence of the modern notion of "history" itself — as an academic discipline, rather than a spiritual "text" from which to extract eternal lessons to apply to the present. Gilmore points, as an example of this, to the late sixteenth-century shift in the study of law, from a focus on the present-day application of ancient rules to the study of classical law as a particular historical product (p. 97). He connects this shift to a movement away from the notion that ideas have "universal validity" to an understanding of the uniqueness of the formulations of particular periods. And, indeed, it is in this era that the first real "histories" — in the modern sense of the word, as the description of distinct periods — begin to be written (Weiss, 137), as also begins what Ariès calls the "sixteenth-century passion for dating," for example, portraits, furniture, silverware, and glasses. Most published works, too, began to be inscribed with the author's age, or the date and place of the author's birth (Ariès, 16–17).

The development of the human sense of locatedness can be viewed as a process of cultural parturition, from which the human being emerges as a decisively separate entity, no longer continuous with a universe which has now become decisively "other" to it. That universe no longer beats with the same heart as the human being; it has its own laws, which control and contain (in both senses of the word) the activity of the self.

It is time for me to raise an important distinction here: that between "locatedness," on the one hand, and what I will call the sense of "place," on the other. The sense of locatedness, as I've described it here, is related to what Whitehead has called "simple location," a notion which he claims "is the very foundation of the seventeenth-century scheme of nature." "Simple location" is the "perfectly definite sense" in which something "can be said to be *here* in space and *here* in time, or *here* in space-time . . . [without] any reference to other regions of space-time" (1925, p. 49). In other words, the "simple location" of something is the location of the thing, considered as an "independent, individual . . . bit of matter" (1933, p. 156). The sense of locatedness is the experience of *oneself* as "simply located."

The sense of "place," on the other hand, is the experience of "fit," of *belonging* where one is, of having a home. It is the assurance that where one is, is appropriate or meaningful or of value within some larger context. One could say that the sense of "place" takes the sting out of the recognition of locatedness. And, indeed, the shock of separation, for the human child, is compensated for (when conditions permit) by the nurturing home provided by the parents, by their continued assurance that the place occupied by the newborn is a privileged and secure one, that the newly emerged entity has not been thrust into a world indifferent to it.

In the historical period in question, on the cultural level, no such assurance was to be had. For, infinity had "opened its jaws" and the medieval universe — once "as safely enclosed as a cot in the nursery or a babe in the womb" (Koestler, 19) — had been burst asunder. Many authors consider this, and not the "Copernican Revolution," to have been the most profound result of the scientific transformations of the modern era. The heliocentric system may have meant a demotion of the earth's significance in the cosmic system, but the change from a heliocentric to an acentric system raised a more radically disturbing possibility, namely, that there is no intelligible cosmic system at all, no center of orientation, and, therefore, no spiritually proper "home" for anything. The medieval universe had been not only a limited but a *centered* universe, with a core toward which all movement tended. Both of these were significant "horizons" for the medieval experience of the world. The sense of limitless *distance* that we experience, C. S. Lewis and Barfield suggest, was simply not there.

> [In the medieval experience] the earth is really the centre, really the lowest place; movement to it from whatever direction is downward movement. As a modern, you locate the stars at a great distance. For distance you must now substitute that very special, and far less abstract, sort of distance which we

call height; height, which speaks immediately to our muscles and nerves . . .
because the medieval universe is finite, it has a shape, the perfect spherical
shape . . . to look out on the night sky with modern eyes is like looking out
over a sea that fades away into a mist, or looking about one in a trackless
forest — trees forever and no horizon. To look out at the towering medieval
universe is much more like looking at a great building . . . Pascal's terror at
le silence éternal de ces espaces infinis never entered [the medieval's] mind. He
is like a man being conducted through an immense cathedral, not like one
lost on a shoreless sea (Lewis, 98–100).

If it were daytime, we see the air filled with light proceeding from a living
sun, rather as our own flesh is filled with blood proceeding from a living
heart. If it is nighttime, we do not merely see a plain, homogeneous vault
pricked with separate regions of light, but a regional, qualitative sky, from
which first of all the different sections of the great zodiacal belt, and second-
ly the planets and the moon . . . are raying down their complex influences
upon the earth, its metals, its plants, its animals, including ourselves . . . .
As to the planets themselves, without being especially interested in astrology,
we know very well that growing things are specially beholden to the sun,
that gold and silver draw their virtue from sun and moon respectively, cop-
per from Venus, iron from Mars, lead from Saturn. And that our own
health and temperament are joined by invisible threads to these heavenly
bodies we are looking at (Barfield, 46–47).

The postulation of infinity, on the other hand, had made the notion of
a core unintelligible. The universe was now not only limitless but "decen-
tralized, perplexing and anarchic" (Koestler, 217).[10] This, says Gillispie, was
a "deeper philosophical disorientation than any other." Without a core, there
is no center of orientation. And without a center of orientation, there is "no
place in nature where man specifically belongs" (p. 84). Indeed, there is no
such thing as *place* at all.

There can be no place — no proper "home" — but there *is* "simple location."

> . . . if a region is merely a way of indicating a certain set of relations to
> other entities, then this characteristic, which I call simple location, is that
> material can be said to have just these relations of position to the other
> entites without requiring for its explanation any reference to other regions
> constituted by analogous relations of position to the same entities. In fact, as
> soon as you have settled, however you do settle, what you mean by a
> definite place in space-time, you can adequately state the relation of a par-
> ticular material body to space-time by saying that it is just there, in that
> place; and, so far as simple location is concerned, there is nothing more to
> be said on the subject (Whitehead, 1925, p. 49).

That "nothing more" is the essence of Pascal's dread. In the Aristotelian universe — which, as Barfield, Berman and Lewis suggest, was in many ways the experiential as well as the theoretical universe of the Middle Ages — *place* is not only the "ecological niche" proper to each thing (Green, 158), but has "a certain influence" over the thing: "each [of the elementary natural bodies] is carried to its own place, if it is not hindered" (Aristotle, *Physics*, 208b10); for example, the heavy toward the center of the cosmos, the light away from it. Locatedness, contrastingly, is experienced by Pascal as an arbitrary and impersonal "allotment": "There is no reason for me to be here rather than there, now rather than then. Who put me here?" And, indeed, "here" considered in larger terms — as the "here" of the human home, the earth — had no longer a spiritual or cosmological place in the universe. As in Donne's famous poem, that earth is now "lost," and "no mans wit Can well direct him, where to looke for it."

"For what is our Globe but a Point, a Trifle to the Universe!" exclaims Derham (Lovejoy, 134), a macrocosmic expression of Pascal's despair at the insignificance of his own "small space" on earth, "swallowed up in the infinite immensity of spaces of which I know nothing and which know nothing of me." The imagery of locatedness — the metaphors of "point," "space," "allotment of place" — are in such expressions combined with the imagery of homelessness, abandonment, the apprehension of almost personal, willful indifference on the part of the universe.

This cold, indifferent universe, and the newly separate self "simply located" within it, form the experiential context for Cartesian epistemological anxiety as much as for Pascal's more existential response. We have seen how such anxiety manifests itself in the *Meditations* in a heightened sense of the interiority and enclosedness of experience within the subject, and a sense of profound distance between self and world. We have also seen how the threat of relativism and perspectivism — deriving from the new cultural sense of cognitive locatedness, of the limits of the "point of view" — is at the heart of Cartesian doubt.

Yet the very same elements that produce anxiety — the barrenness of the universe, the separateness of self and world — are precisely those that are turned, by Descartes, to the greatest epistemological advantage, as we will see in the next essay. "Descartes," says Charles Gillispie, "felt no compunction about turning man loose in an infinite universe, so long as his own ideas were clear and simple" (p. 89). In the next essay, I will explore the strategy that Descartes employs to convert the anxieties spoken of in this and preceding essays into the certitude of objectivity.

Chapter Five

PURIFICATION AND TRANSCENDENCE IN DESCARTES'S MEDITATIONS

> Me-thinks, I see how all the old Rubbish must be thrown away, and the rotten Buildings be overthrown, and carried away with so powerful an Inundation. These are the days that must lay a new foundation of a more magnificent Philosophy, never to be overthrown . . . a true and permanent Philosophy.
>
> Henry Power, *Experimental Philosophy*

CARTESIANISM AND THE QUEST FOR PURITY

Where there is anxiety, there will almost certainly be found a mechanism of defense against that anxiety. In *Pensées*, VI, 113, Pascal expresses, in one line, what might be seen as the *modus operandi* for the modern struggle for control over the sense of arbitrary allotment of time and place within an indifferent, alien universe. "*Through space*," he says, "*the universe grasps me and swallows me up like a speck; through thought I grasp it.*" If the impersonal, arbitrary universe of the early modern era is capable of physically "swallowing" him, like a random bit of ontological debris, *he* is nonetheless capable of containing and subduing it — through comprehension, through the "grasp" of the mind. As in much of early modern science and philosophy — in Bacon, most dramatically — the dream of knowledge is here imagined as an explicit revenge fantasy, an attempt to wrest back control from nature.

The fantasy of absolute understanding, of course, motivated Descartes much more than Pascal. But the thought through which Descartes conquered the indifferent, infinite universe was a thought very different from that imagined in Pascal's *Pensées*. To *comprehend* — to contain the whole within the grasp of the mind — is simply not possible for a finite intelligence, as Descartes makes clear.[1] Rather, what seizes the Cartesian imagination is

75

the possibility of *pure* thought, of *pure* perception. Such perception, far from embracing the whole, demands the disentangling of the various objects of knowledge *from* the whole of things, and beaming a light on the essential separateness of each — its own pure and discrete nature, revealed as *it* is, free of the "distortions" of subjectivity. Arithmetic and geometry are natural models for the science that will result; for, as Descartes says, they "alone deal with an object so pure and uncomplicated, that they need make no assumptions at all which experience renders uncertain" (*Regulae*, HR, I, 5). The "intuitions" of the *Regulae*, the "simples" of the *Discourse*, and the clear and distinct perceptions of the *Meditations* are attempts to describe the possibility of such objects for philosophy, a class of "privileged representations," as Rorty puts it, "so compelling that their accuracy cannot be doubted." Much of Meditation IV, I will argue, turns on the delineation of such a class of ideas.

For these "privileged representations" to reveal themselves, the knower must be purified, too — of all bias, all "perspective," all emotional attachment. And for Descartes, this necessarily involves the transcendence of the body, not only of the "prejudices" acquired through the body-rule of infancy but of all the bodily distractions and passions that obscure our thinking. The *Meditations*, I propose, should be read as providing a guide and exemplar of such bodily transcendence.

The result for Descartes is a new model of knowledge, grounded in *objectivity*, and capable of providing a new epistemological security to replace that which was lost in the dissolution of the medieval world-view. It is a model that, although under attack, is still largely with analytic philosophy today, and that still revolves around the imagery of *purity*. Locke spoke of philosophy as removing the "rubbish lying in the way of knowledge." Three centuries later, Quine wrote that the task of the philosopher was "clearing the ontological slums" (p. 275). The image of the philosopher as tidying the mess left by others is more subtly presented by Arthur Danto, who views the philosopher as "executing the tasks of conceptual housekeeping [the sciences and other disciplines] are too robustly busy to tend to themselves" (p. 10).

The creation of a "pure" realm, untouched by uncertainty and risk, always necessitates, as Dewey points out (p. 8), the designation of a contrastingly "impure" realm to absorb or take responsibility for the messy aspects of experience. In the history of philosophy, the role of the unclean and the impure has been played, variously, by material reality, practical activity, change, the emotions, "subjectivity," and most often — as for Descartes — by the *body*. In Locke and Danto's conception of philosophy, the other disciplines play this role: They are the earth to philosophy's spirit, the "matter" to philosophy's "form", providing the "stuff" to be analyzed, organized and corrected by philosophy's purifying scrutiny.[2]

What makes such conceptions peculiarly Cartesian is not just their implicit assumption that the philosopher is in possession of some neutral "matrix" (as Rorty calls it) with which to perform an ultimate critical or conceptual cleansing, but their passion for intellectual separation, demarcation, and *order*. The other disciplines, as Feyerabend says, must be "tamed [and put] in their place" (p. 21); their "robust" effort is fine, so long as there is someone specifically charged to clean up the conceptual debris left in its wake.

Rorty is critical of this conception of the role of the philosopher, according to which the philosopher occupies a space, not within the cultural conversation, but removed, at a distance, linguistically interpreting, logically overseeing, and epistemologically scrutinizing the proceedings. The pretension to do so is not only professionally hubristic, insisting as it does that the philosopher's voice "always has an overriding claim on the attention of other participants in the conversation" (p. 392), but is based on a profound self-deception. For Rorty, the belief that one may lay claim to an ultimate critical framework of any sort is illusory, an attempt to "escape from history," context, and human finitude (p. 9). Rorty here places himself firmly within the Nietzschean and Deweyan "therapeutic" traditions in philosophy, for whom the intellectual hunger for purity, clarity, and order is revealed to have an "underside" — in the desire for control over the more unruly, "cthonic" dimensions of experience. The sociologist Richard Sennett, too, has described what he calls the "purification urge" — toward ordering the world according to firm, clearly articulated categories permitting of no ambiguity and dissonance — as "the desire to be all-powerful, to control the meanings of experience before encounter so as not to be overwhelmed" (p. 116). Against any possibile threat to that organization, strict rules against mixing categories or blurring boundaries must be maintained. The ontological order must be clear and distinct. The anthropologist Mary Douglas has argued that maintaining such pristine ontological integrity — "keeping distinct the categories of creation . . . [through] correct definition, discrimination and order" — animates religious conceptions of purity (1966, p. 53). For the Cartesian, too, ambiguity and contradiction are the worst transgressions. That which cannot be categorized cleanly deserves no place in the universe.

For Descartes, the quest for purity of thought serves more historically specific mechanisms, as well. For, the alien, impersonal nature of the infinite universe — that wasteland of meaninglessness, that terrifying, cold expanse — is precisely what allows it to be known with precision, clarity, and detachment. In a universe in which the spiritual and the physical merge, where body and mind participate in knowledge, objectivity is impossible. (And, in such a world, objectivity is not an ideal.) The quest for objectivity, on the other hand, is capable of transforming the barren landscape of the modern universe into a paradise for analysis, dissection, and "controlled" experimentation. Its barrenness, which filled Pascal with such existential dread, is, of course, precisely what makes it capable of being "read" mathematically and taken apart with philosophical accuracy — and moral impunity.

THE PURIFICATION OF THE UNDERSTANDING

At the start of the fourth Meditation, Descartes finds himself on the horns of the dilemma. The proof of the existence of a veracious God has insured him that he is not the victim of a systematic deception and — what amounts to the same thing — that his own capacity for judgment, "doubtless received from God," will not "lead me to err if I use it aright" (HR, I, 172). Yet, of course, we *do* err. How to reconcile this fallibility with his newly established faith in the veracity of God and the fitness of his own faculties?

Descartes, to begin with, considers several solutions of a traditional nature. He first considers that his own nature, not being God-like, but rather somewhere "between the supreme Being and non-being," must "in some degree participate . . . in nought or in non-being." He should not be surprised therefore to find in himself, in addition to the positive faculties given to him by God, *defects* in those faculties. Error need not be attributed to "a special faculty given me by God"; rather, "I fall into error from the fact that the power given me by God for the purpose of distinguishing truth from error is not infinite" (HR, I, 172–3).

But this answer does not satisfy Descartes, "for error is not a pure negation [i.e., is not the simple defect or want of some perfection which ought not to be mine], but it is a lack of some knowledge which it seems I ought to possess" (HR, I, 173). And the seeming failure of God to bestow on me an understanding that would be without such a lack requires explanation.

Perhaps, however, my intellectual defects serve higher ends. It is not, after all, within my capacity to understand all of God's design; for all I know, my own imperfections when considered as "part of the whole universe" are "very perfect." (HR, I, 173). This explanation is not rejected by Descartes, but he does not go any further with it. It appears to function, rather, as a "tradi-tionalist" prelude to what will turn out to be a decidedly innovative approach to the problem of error.

The form of that new approach, like many of Descartes's most radical departures from scholasticism, is itself traditional — an epistemological variant of the Augustinian "solution" to the problem of evil. For Augustine, "God made man but not the sin in him": Human evil is the result of our capacity for free will — given to us by God, and itself good — but mean-ingless unless the choice of evil is a real possibility. Freedom is not freedom if it is determined to choose the good; in "allowing" us to sin, God is not responsible for evil but for giving us the capacity to behave as moral agents. The will alone is responsible for sin.

Descartes's strategy for dealing with the "problem of error" corresponds to Augustine's approach to the problem of evil. As, for Augustine, God is absolved and the human being charged with sole responsibility for moral fallenness, so, for Descartes, the human being is charged with all responsi-bility for *epistemological* "fallenness":

> ... it is not an imperfection in God that He has given me the liberty to give or withhold my assent from certain things as to which He has not placed a clear and distinct knowledge in my understanding; but it is without doubt an imperfection in me not make good use of my freedom, and to give my judgment readily on matters which I only understand obscurely (HR, I, 177).

It is important to note that judgment here is conceived as an act distinct from the act of understanding. For, "by the understanding alone I [neither assert nor deny anything, but] apprehend the ideas of things as to which I can form a judgement" (HR, I, 174). Judgment is rather an act of the will, as Descartes makes clear in the *Notes Directed Against a Certain Programme*:

> ... I saw that, over and above perception, which is required as a basis for judgment, there must needs be affirmation, or negation, to constitute the form of the judgment, and that it is frequently open to us to withhold our assent, even if we perceive a thing. I referred the act of judging, which con-sists in nothing but *assent*, i.e., affirmation or negation, not to the perception of the understanding, but to the determination of the will (HR, I, 446).

Errors, therefore, are acts of the will, or, more precisely, acts of misuse of the will. The way they occur is the following: Although the faculty of will, like the understanding, is "perfect of its kind," being "much wider in its range and compass than the understanding," it sometimes gives its assent to "things which I do not understand" (HR, I, 175). This assent to the obscure or confused represents a misuse of the will, for "the light of nature teaches us that the knowledge of the understanding should always precede the determination of the will" (HR, I 177; see also *Principle* XLIII, I, 236).

The conception of judgment as an act of will rather than intellect (a radical departure from scholastic tradition), is essential to Descartes's epistemological program in several ways.

1. It is essential to the comprehensibility of Cartesian doubt. For, the methodical "abstent[ion] from giving assent to dubious things" that is Cartesian doubt *is* an act of will rather than intellect. It is an attitude chosen prior to any particular intellectual act, and (even though undertaken to confront a *real* skeptical threat, as I have suggested in essay one) is deliberately chosen as a route to that goal.

2. As suggested earlier, it exonerates God from the responsibility for error, just as, for Augustine, the attribution of sin to human will exonerates God from the responsibility of having created evil. As such, it is actually the final (though not explicitly presented as such) stage in the full proof of the existence of a veracious God. For, how can I reconcile the veracity of God with the fact of human error? Unless the responsibility for error can be shown to lie elsewhere, the image, if not of an evil genius, then at least of a less than totally veracious God, again could undercut our newly won confidence in our facilities. But since error is the result, instead, of the *wrong use* which we make of the humanly *perfect* faculties given to us by God, the responsibility for it is all ours — and within our control.

3. It serves as an argument for the purity of the understanding. The above correspondence between Descartes's treatment of error and the traditional handling of the "problem of evil" was first described by Etienne Gilson[3] and is ascribed to, in passing, by J. L. Evans (p. 137), Bernard Williams (p. 169), and Hiram Caton (p. 90). The way this correspondence has been formulated, however, has missed something whose significance is crucial to understanding the fourth Meditation. All emphasis, in Gilson's account, has been placed on the exoneration of *God* from the charge of responsibility for error — which indeed is stressed by Descartes, and which is the obvious keynote comparsion to be made *if* the "problem of error" is taken to be *symmetrically* correspondent with the solution to the problem of evil. But it is not symmetrically correspondent. In the context of the problem of evil, the traditional arguments exonerate God alone, not also the will. Whereas, in the context of the problem of intellectual error, on the other hand, in exonerating God, Descartes also exonerated the intellect itself, and

not incidentally.[4] In relocating error "outside" the understanding, Descartes is not only placing it in the province of the will, but purging the understanding of what stands in the way of *its* perfection. It therefore counts as an argument for the purity of the understanding as much as an argument for the goodness of God.

The difference is crucial, not only to clarification of the arguments which follow in the *Meditations*, and to our understanding of the overall project of the *Meditations*, but to our understanding of the philosophical and cultural reconstruction within which Descartes plays such a central role. What we are enabled to see, *in process* as it were, is a historical movement away from a transcendent God as the only legitimate object of worship to the establishing of the *human intellect* as godly, and as appropriately to be revered and submitted to — once "purified" of all that stands in the way of its godliness. Shortly, for modern science, God will indeed become downright superfluous. In the *Meditations*, God most certainly is not. But God's role in that work nonetheless almost approaches the metaphorical: Just as the Evil Genius functions as a personification of the possibility of radical defect in the human faculties of knowing, so a veracious God seems a personification of faith in those faculties. That Descartes's strategy for exonerating God for error is *simultaneously* a strategy for purifying the understanding is suggestive of a merging of foci here. The godly intellect is on the way to becoming the true deity of the modern era.

That Descartes employs an epistemological variant of a traditional solution to the "problem of evil" suggests that *purification* is not too strong a term to describe his project for certifying the perfection of the intellect. The project to conceptually purify one realm, as noted earlier, necessitates a "relocation" of all threatening elements "outside." They become *alien.* This is the strategy employed by Augustine in his answer to the problem of evil, as William James points out in *The Varieties of Religious Experience.* There, James argues that the construal of evil as a "problem" for which God must be absolved of responsibility necessitates transforming "an essential part of our being" into "a waste element, to be sloughed off . . . diseased, inferior, excrementitious stuff" (p. 129).

The strategy, as Mary Douglas points out, is the same, in form and function, as that of social rituals of purification, in which a society establishes some substance or group as impure and "taboo," thus "defining" it as outside the social body. Insuring that the tabooed thing or group remains separate and does not contaminate the social body sometimes requires violent expulsions, as in witch hunting (1982, pp. 107–124). But usually the taboo functions through the establishment of separate metaphysical "realms" — a good "inside" and a bad "outside" — as, pursuing this analogy, it does for Descartes. Error is not extinguished, but excluded; it is conceptualized as belonging outside an inner circle of purity, in this case, the godly intellect.

Douglas suggests the term "dirt-rejecting" for those philosophers who pursue such purification strategies (1966, p. 164). In terms of such a category, Descartes is an epistemological "dirt-rejecter." Not that he doesn't see confusion and obscurity everywhere ("smudges on the mirror of nature," as a colleague has described it) — for he does. But his entire system is devoted to circumscribing an intellectual arena which is pristinely immune to contamination, a mirror which is impossible to smudge. Here, we should recall the Cartesian imagery of mistaken ideas as spoiled and rotting fruit, capable of corrupting everything that comes into contact with them. Error can no longer be conceptualized as a negation by Descartes (as the medievals had been able to do). For the culture he lived in, unlike the medieval world, uncertainty and confusion seemed so ubiquitous as to suggest that human nature may have been malevolently (or at least mischievously) *designed* to err, as we saw in essay two. But error can be reconceptualized as "belonging" to a faculty other than the intellect (just as evil had been conceived as belonging to *us*, rather than God). In this way the first step is made toward preparing the intellect to enter into a pure, "godly" relation with its objects of knowledge.

PASSIVITY AND TRUTH

Descartes's initial "purification of the understanding" is, however, *only* a first step. For, the intellect has not quite been purged of all the elements lying in the way of its purity. Denial, assertion, desiring, aversion, and doubting have all become the province of the will. Only the "acts of understanding" — perceiving, imagining, conceiving — remain the province of the understanding. In Meditation III, Descartes had described these as the only forms to which the title "idea" should be properly applied, because they alone do not "add something else to the idea which I have of the thing" (HR, I, 159). They are, in other words, *representations*. And, as such, they may of course *mis*represent. Therein lies the problem. If the faculty of judgment is free (as at this point it seems to be) to accept or reject the claims of the ideas that it surveys that they represent the state of things, what is to prevent us from constantly falling into error? The ideas that "pass in review" (to borrow Rorty's phrase) before the "inner eye" of judgment are, after all, a motley array. They include both perceptions that are the result of the acts of volition (imaginatively constructed entities, intelligible objects) and "passive" perceptions, "receive[d] from the things represented by them" (*Passions of the Soul*, HR, I, 340). The latter include the perceptions that occur within dreams and daydreams, bodily perceptions such as pain, heat and cold, the emotions ("the passions of the soul"), and the perceptions of external objects. This is a diverse assemblage, a real democracy of inner representations, united by their common relation to the "inner arena" — the soul — which Descartes likens to the relation between the shapes a piece of wax may take and the wax itself.

> It receives its ideas partly from objects in contact with the senses, partly from impressions in the brain, and partly from precedent dispositions in the soul and motions of the will. Similarly, a piece of wax owes its shapes partly to the pressure of other bodies, partly to its own earlier shape or other qualities such as heaviness and softness, and partly also to its own movement, when, having been pushed it has in itself the power to continue moving (To Mesland, May 2, 1644; PL, 148).

In this analogy, the suggestion is that all our ideas have equal power to impress themselves on the intellect. But for Descartes, the intellect is not quite the democracy of ideas suggested by the analogy with wax. For some ideas are aristocrats and have the power to compel the assent of the will.

> For example, when I lately examined whether anything existed in the world, and found that from the very fact that I considered this question it followed very clearly that I myself existed, I could not prevent myself from believing that a thing I so clearly conceived was true: not that I found myself compelled to do so by some external cause, but simply because from great clearness in my mind there followed a great inclination of my will . . . (Meditation IV, HR, I, 176).
>
> The will of a thinking thing is borne, willingly indeed and freely (for that is the essense of the will), but none the less infallibly, toward the good that it clearly knows (Reply II, HR, II, 56).
>
> For it seems to me certain that *a great light in the intellect is followed by a strong inclination in the will*; so that if we see very clearly that a thing is good for us it is very difficult — and, on my view, impossible, as long as one continues in the same thought — to stop the course of our desire (to Mesland, May 2, 1644; PL, 149).

We are free, to be sure, to cease to *attend* to our clear and distinct perceptions (from this comes the fact that we "earn merit" for the good acts that follow "infallibility" from those perceptions), but to choose to attend is to immediately "ensure that our will follows so promptly the light of our understanding that there is no longer in any way indifference" (to Mesland, PL, 150).[6]

On closer inspection, indeed, it turns out that there is, in fact, only *one* way in which the judgment can *err*: by giving assent to the obscure and confused. This limitation on error runs throughout the Cartesian corpus, from the *Regulae*, which instructs us "never to assume what is false is true" (HR, I, 9), but does not mention the converse, to the *Principles*: "We deceive ourselves *only* when we form judgments about anything insufficiently known to us" (HR, I, 232). And, of course, in the *Meditations*:

> Whence then come my errors? They come from the sole fact that . . . I do not restrain [the will] within [the bounds of the understanding], but extend it also to things which I do not understand: and as the will is of itself indifferent to these, it easily falls into error and sin, and chooses the evil for the good, or the false for the true (HR, I, Meditation IV, 175-176).

In the above quotation, what Descartes calls the "understanding" is *identified* with the capacity to *correctly* (i.e., clearly and distinctly) understand, rather than with the general faculty of receiving, recalling, or combining ideas. His inconsistency is not my focus here, however. What is important is that a new mental arena has been designated, one which is normatively delineated — by the qualities of clearness and distinctness. And the capacity to fall into error has been circumscribed as well. It is connected, not with the freedom of the will but with the *indifference* of the will. These, for Descartes, are two very different things. To explain this will require some sorting out of the Cartesian doctrine of the will: the faculty of will itself is simply

> the power of choosing to do a thing or not to do it (that is, to affirm or deny, to pursue or to shun it), or rather it consists alone in the fact that in order to affirm or deny, pursue or shun those things placed before us by the understanding, we act so that we are unconscious that any outside force constrains us in doing so (Meditation IV, HR, I, 175).

It is important to note that for Descartes the power of the will to choose a course of action is not simply "negative" freedom — is not simply the absence of force or constraint on our actions — a "freedom" shared by animals, who do not *will* their activities, and who cannot therefore be said to be truly "free" (to Mesland, PL, 150). Rather, the power of the will is the "positive faculty of determining oneself to one or other of two contraries" (to Mesland, February 9, 1645; PL, 161), the power, in other words, of acting *voluntarily* (and not merely automatically or instinctually).

Within this general freedom, Descartes notes, there are different grades of freedom. The highest — the "greater liberty," as Descartes calls it — consists in one of two things: *either* "a great faculty in determining oneself" through "follow[ing] the course which appears to have the most reasons in its favor" *or* "a greater use of the positive power which we have of following the worse, although we see the better" (to Mesland, PL, 160). The latter refers to those special cases when we "hold back from pursuing a clearly known good, or from admitting a clearly perceived truth [because] we consider it a good thing to demonstrate the freedom of our will by doing so" (to Mesland, PL, 160). The former reconciles the *freedom* of the will with the will's assent to the clear and distinct perception. Indeed, Descartes affirms that the "greater the inclination of the will" that follows from the "clearness of the mind," the "greater [the] freedom or spontaneity" of the act (Meditation IV, HR, I, 176).

This reconciliation is similar to the reconciliation of determinism and freedom offered by so-called "soft determinists," who replace the traditional opposition between these two with an opposition between freedom and external compulsion. For the soft determinist, I am free, not insofar as my actions are *undetermined*, but insofar as they are determined by my *own* inclinations rather than an external force. And for Descartes, indeed, the "lowest degree of liberty" is *indifference*: the state in which nothing in the self determines us to any direction, when the will "is not impelled one way rather than another by any perception of truth or goodness" (to Mesland, PL, 159).

The capacity to err derives, as we have seen, from this state of indifference. Correspondingly, when we *cannot* maintain indifference — when we are irresistibly drawn to one side rather than another — we can be assured that we are in the presence of truth.

The Cartesian clear and distinct perception is very like an emotion (as emotions are conceived by Descartes) in its capacity to *overtake* us, to absorb us, to render us passive in the face of its strength. But while the emotions may overtake us in ways that obscure our intellectual vision (that is, in the traditional picture that comes down to us from Descartes), the clear and distinct idea overtakes the propensity to error itself. *Our* very passivity in the face of a clear and distinct idea is the mark of *its* truth.

Passivity in the face of an idea — the inability to say "no" to an idea — is a hallmark of epistemological reassurance to one degree or another throughout the *Meditations*. We encounter it first in the fleeting moments of the first and second Meditations when the pull of the clear and distinct perception temporarily subdues doubt. Even *before* it is demonstrated that "all that I know clearly is true," "my mind is such that I could not prevent myself from holding [my perception] to be true so long as I conceive them clearly" (HR, I, 180). This passivity, however, is not to be trusted, for my mind may be such, too, that it is fundamentally flawed, and responds to the false as though it were true (HR, I, 184). I need to be assured that I may trust my own responses (that God has not created me such that I am systematically deceived) before I can take them as guides to the truth of things.

The *cogito*, too, is a case — though a special one — of an idea that compels assent. It is special, as I have argued in essay one, because it is one of a very small class of ideas whose denial, paradoxically, involves assent. It is more resilient to doubt, therefore, than other clear and distinct perceptions, since even if I am sure that my mind is fundamentally flawed, I am still "sure," that is, *thinking* something. But the compelling nature of the *cogito*, in any case, does not assure me that the compelling nature of all other clear and distinct ideas will "as a general rule" insure me of their truth.

For that assurance Descartes needs God. And he needs, in addition (and what amounts to the same thing, but in an "epistemological" form that is a working model of *knowing*), to be assured that we will not be drawn to error in submitting to the force of the intellect. This is what the fourth Meditation accomplishes: *first*, by identifying (if somewhat inconsistently) the intellect with the arena of the clear and distinct, and *second*, by attributing error, not just to the will, but to the *indifferent* will. The will that is compelled by the intellect can never err.

Now the passivity of the soul can be more fully trusted, and we may let our ideas "speak to us," attending to those we can answer and those we cannot. In Meditation IV, for example, the following argument occurs, in which the fact that our perceptions of external objects are not subject to voluntary control turns out to be a strong reason for believing that they proceed from the things they seem to represent.

> There is certainly further in me a certain passive faculty of perception, that is, of receiving and recognizing the ideas of sensible things, but this would be useless to me ... if there were not either in me or in some other thing another active faculty capable of forming and producing these ideas. But this active faculty cannot exist in me ... seeing that it does not presuppose thought, and also that those ideas are often produced in me without my contributing in any way to the same, and often even against my will; it is thus necessarily the case that the faculty resides in some substance different from me in which all the reality which is objectively in the ideas that are produced by this faculty is formally or eminently contained, as I remarked before (HR, I, 191).

This argument does not differ significantly from the argument that Descartes recalls from his naive, pre-doubting days:

> . . . It was not without reason that I believed myself to perceive objects quite different from my thought, to wit, bodies from which those ideas proceeded; for I found by experience that these ideas presented themselves to me without my consent being requisite, so that I could not perceive any object, however desirous I might be, unless it were present to the organs of sense; and it was not in my power not to perceive it, when it was present (HR, I, 187–188).

The difference is not a difference in argument, but a difference in self-trust. Prior to the proofs of God and the account of error, even the strongest natural inclination may be looked on as suspect, once the immediacy of the moment has passed.

> For since nature *seemed* to cause me to lean towards many things from which reason repelled me, I did not believe that I should trust much to the teachings of nature. And although the ideas which I receive by the senses do not depend on my will, I did not think that one should for that reason conclude that they proceeded from things different from myself, since possibly some faculty might be discovered in me — though hitherto unknown to me — which produced them (HR, I, 189; emphasis added).

The qualification "seemed to" is important, for the fourth Meditation has established that this "seeming" was an illusion — that error is always the result of indifference (allowed for only by the obscure and confused perception) and not of real inclination. It is significant, too, that Descartes says that his new-found self-trust is the result, not just of knowing "more clearly the author of my being," but of "know[ing] myself better" (HR, I, 189). The latter was the point of the fourth Meditation — to translate my knowledge that this is God's world into a new model of the human intellect. This new model is one in which indifference rather than inclination is the hallmark of error, and in which, therefore, a class of "godly" ideas — "king," as Dewey puts it, "to any beholding mind that may gaze upon it" (p.23) — could reign supreme. Having attributed judgment to the will, for Descartes it is doubly imperative to circumscribe a set of realities within the intellect that are capable of bending judgment to their authority. The very last thing that Descartes would want is a Jamesian "will to believe," in which the belief in truth itself is "but a passionate affirmation of desire," and behind every particular intellectual position lies "fear and hope, prejudice and passion" (1897, p. 9). Objective evidence and certainty may be "fine ideals to play with," says James, "but where on this moonlit and dream-visited planet are they found?" (p. 14);

"Pretend as we may, the whole man within us is at work when we form our philosophical opinions" (p. 92). The clear and distinct idea, on the contrary, assures us that it is precisely when we form our philosophical opinions that the "whole man" may be *passified* — quite literally — by the purity and authority of the object.

This is, of course, no new theme in the history of philosophy, which is studded with metaphors suggesting spectatorship rather than participation, the "known" specifically conceived as that realm in which the distorting effects of human interest and activity are eliminated, and in which fixity and purity thus rule. But before the sixteenth and seventeenth centuries, such conceptions had been reserved for the sort of knowing that has formal, immutable, or immaterial "reality" as its object. It is only with Descartes that fixity and purity — "the immutable state of mind" — began to be demanded of the knowledge necessary to certify concrete perceptions of the self (that I have hands, eyes, senses, etc.), of particular "corporeal things" (other animals, inanimate things) and, indeed, of *anything* external to consciousness. And it is only in the sixteenth and seventeenth centuries that earthly science, insofar as it is trustworthy, is equated with "spectatorship" and the passive reception of ideas.[7] It is in the work of Descartes that we find the official philosophical birth of the notion of mind as "mirror of nature."

THE TRANSCENDENCE OF THE BODY

The Cartesian purification of the understanding, at this point, is still abstract and conceptual — not methodological. How does one do it? Some *method* of purification must be supplied, some rules to direct the understanding. On this score, of course, Descartes is emphatic: We must learn *how* to achieve the proper sort of receptivity to ideas. And although all persons are capable of learning this, "there are very few who rightly distinguish between what is really perceived and what they fancy they perceive, because but few are accustomed to clear and distinct perceptions" (Reply VII, HR, II, 307).

Descartes recognizes that people may be wrong about what they take to be the clearness and distinctness of ideas. He has even proven himself guilty of it at various points in the progress of the *Meditations*. He agrees with Gassendi that without a method "which will direct and show us when we are in error and when not, so often as we think we clearly and distinctly perceive anything" (HR, II, 152), we are thrown back on each individual's sense of conviction, a psychological datum that cannot be trustworthy in all cases. But, then, in which cases, and for what reasons is testimony to personal conviction trustworthy? The problem is further compounded by the similarities between the workings of the clear and distinct perceptions, which irresistibly dispose the will through the power of intellectual insight, and the emotions, which irresistibly dispose the will through the force of the bodily — the attendant "commotion" in the heart, blood and "animal spirits" which "prevents the soul from being able at one to change or arrest its passions" (HR, I, 352).[8] To be sure, the clear and distinct perception is "seen" with the mind, whereas the emotions are felt by the body. But the issue at stake here is not how to distinguish between the two; rather, what is at issue is the epistemological trustworthiness of the "irresistible" *qua* irresistible: If the will can be overtaken and bent in directions that oppose reason (as it is often by the body [I, 353]), then how can the will's passivity itself serve as a mark that reason has conducted itself to the truth (as it is supposed to via the clear and distinct perception)?

We need to recall now that what principally stands in the way of the "habit" of clear and distinct perception (taken as an activity now, rather than a content or object) is what Descartes generally calls "prejudice," but which, on closer inspection, turns out to be a specific sort of prejudice — that of "seeing" with one's *body* rather than one's *mind*. This, as we have seen, is the original, and most formidable legacy of infancy, a time in which the mind, "newly united" to the body, was "wholly occupied in perceiving or feeling the ideas of pain, pleasure, heat, cold and other similar ideas which arise from its union and intermingling with the body" (to Hyperaspistes, August 1641, PL 111). "The body is always a hindrance to the mind in its thinking," he tells Burman, "and this was especially true in youth" (B, 8).

That Descartes views the "prison of the body" as the chief, if not sole, source of our inability to perceive clearly and distinctly is evidenced by a remarkable passage in the letter to Hyperaspistes, in which Descartes maintains that the infant "has in itself the ideas of God, itself, and all such truths as are called self-evident . . . if it were taken out of the prison of the body it would find [those ideas] within itself" (PL, 111). That this "prison" can, in fact, be transcended in adulthood is no less in doubt for Descartes.

> Nothing in metaphysics causes more trouble than the making the perception of its primary notions clear and distinct. For, though in their own nature they are as intelligible as, or even more intelligible than those the geometricians study, yet being contradicted by the many preconceptions of our senses to which we have since our earliest years been accustomed, they cannot be perfectly apprehended *except by those who give strenuous attention and study to them, and withdraw their minds as far as possible from matters corporeal* (Reply II, HR, II, 49–50; emphasis added).

In *The Passions of the Soul*, Descartes explicitly opposes his own view —
that the body is the source of all in us that is "opposed to reason" — to the
traditional view that it is the inferior, appetitive, or sensuous part of the soul
itself that wars with the rational (HR, I, 353). He is thus able, given the "real
distinction between soul and body" (see *Principle* LX, HR, I, 243; Meditation
VI, HR, I, 190; *Discourse*, HR, I, 101; to Reneri, April 1638, PL, 52) to conceptualize the possibility of complete intellectual transcendence of the appetitive
and sensuous. Although the soul "can have its operations disturbed by the
bad disposition of the bodily organs" (PL, 52) or the passions, "even those
who have the feeblest souls can acquire a very absolute dominion over all
their passions if sufficient industry is applied in training and guiding them"
(*Passions*, HR, I, 356).

Such "training" is largely a matter of accumulating, in the moments
when the soul's operations are undisturbed, a strong arsenal of rational truth
to rely on when agitation threatens. The resolution to carry out what reason
recommends, at such time, is the essence of human happiness, as Descartes
tells Elizabeth (August 4, 1645, PL, 165). When Elizabeth (quite understand-
ably) expressed skepticism over this, pointing out that there are diseases that
overpower the faculty of reason "and with it the satisfaction proper to a
rational mind," Descartes confidently replied that repetition is the key: " . . .
if one often has a certain thought while one's body was at liberty, it returns
again no matter how indisposed the body may be." He himself, he assured
her, had in this way completely eliminated bad dreams from his sleep (PL,
168). He presumably did not notice that they return in the first Meditation.

Not only, however, may the properly trained mind overcome the passions. In certain mental acts, as Margaret Wilson points out (in Hooker, 99),
it actually does "think without the body," as Descartes claims it can in the
letter to Reneri (PL, 52) and in Meditation VI (HR, I, 193). These are the
acts of "pure intellection" or "pure understanding," which not only have no
"imagic" content (e.g., the chiliagon, the idea of God, the idea of a thinking
thing), but no corporeal correlates at all. Unlike sensation, imagery and
memory, acts of "pure understanding" (and the memory of them) are not
only "phenomenologically" independent of the body, but independent of all
physical processes whatever. In a letter to Mesland, for example (PL, 148),
Descartes argues that the memory of intellectual things, unlike those of
material things, depends on "traces" left in thought itself, not in the brain.
And in the Gassendi Replies he states quite emphatically that "I have often
also shown distinctly that mind can act independently of the brain; for certainly the brain can be of no use in pure thought: its only use is for imagining
and perceiving" (HR, I, 212).[9]

To achieve this autonomy, the mind must be gradually liberated from the body: it must *become* a "pure mind." First, constant vigilance must be maintained against the distractions of the body. Throughout the *Meditations*, emphasis is placed on training oneself in nonreliance on the body and practice in the art of "pure understanding." It is virtually a kind of mechanistic yoga.

> I shall now close my eyes, I shall stop my ears, I shall call away all my senses, I shall efface even from my thoughts all the images of corporeal things, or at least (for that is hardly possible) I shall esteem them as vain and false; and thus holding converse only with myself and considering my own nature, I shall try little by little to reach a better knowledge of and a more familiar acquaintanceship with myself (Meditation III, HR, I, 157).

Indeed, much of the *Meditations* may be read as prescribing rules for the liberation of mind from the various seductions of the body, in order to cleanse and prepare it for the reception of clear and distinct ideas. The initial requirement is to "deliver [the] mind from every care . . . and agitat[ion from the] passions" (HR, I, 145). Since, as we have seen, our passionate inclinations can bend the will in directions which oppose reason, it is essential that we not be susceptible to their coercive power while we are pursuing truth. The field must be cleared of such influence, so we will be receptive to the coerciveness exercised by ideas alone.

The next step is to topple the "prejudices" acquired through the body-rule of infancy and childhood. These prejudices have their origin in a hyperabsorption in the senses. But their precise form, as we have seen, is the inability to properly distinguish what is happening solely "inside" the subject from what has an external existence — e.g., the attribution of heat, cold, etc., to the object, of greater "reality" to rocks than water because of their greater heaviness, and so on. As an infant "swamped" inside the body, one simply did not have a perspective from which to discriminate, to judge. In Meditation I, Descartes re-creates that state of utter entrapment, by luring the reader, first, through the continuities between madness and dreaming — that state each night when all of us lose our adult clarity and detachment — and then to the possibility that the whole of our existence may be like a dream, a grand illusion so encompassing that there is no conceivable perspective from which to judge its correspondance with reality. The difference, of course, is that in childhood, we *assumed* that what we felt was a measure of external reality; now, as mature Cartesian doubters, we reverse that prejudice. We assume nothing. We refuse to let our bodies mystify us. And we begin afresh, as pure minds.

This reading of the *Meditations* suggests that a long-standing issue for Cartesian scholars may be founded on a mistake about the nature of Descartes's epistemological program. From Gassendi and Leibniz to Prichard, Ashworth, and Gewirth, commentators have criticized and wrestled with the seeming lack of "objective" criteria for the clearness and distinctness of ideas; with the seeming need for a method, as Gassendi put it, "which will direct and show us when we are in error and when not, so often as we think that we clearly and distinctly perceive anything" (HR, II, 152). Gassendi was struck, as Montaigne had been before him, by the vicissitudes of human certainty and the tenacity with which people may cling to their ever-shifting convictions. He was impressed with, and reminded Descartes of, the number of people willing to die for false beliefs, beliefs that those people presumably perceived as true. Descartes's answer — that he has *supplied* the needed method of discrimination in the procedure of the *Meditations*, "where I first laid aside all prejudices, and afterward enumerated all the chief ideas, distinguishing the clear from the obscure and confused" (HR, II, 214) — did not satisfy Gassendi. It seemed to him to beg the question, like many of Descartes's replies to his critics. Descartes, for his part, was unimpressed with Gassendi's example of those who face death for the sake of (possibly false) opinions, because "it can never be proved that they clearly and distinctly perceive what they pertinaciously affirm" (HR, II, 214). Is Descartes's reasoning hopelessly circular, as Ashworth, following Gassendi, claims (p. 102)?

I would suggest that when Descartes tells Gassendi that he has "attended" to the problem of "finding a method for deciding whether we err or not when we think that we perceive something clearly" (HR, II, 214), he does *not* mean that he believes himself to have supplied criteria for the clearness and distinctness of ideas. He has "attended" to the problem, rather, by supplying "rules for the direction of the mind" (read: rules for the transcendence of the body) that will prepare the mind to be swayed by nothing but the peculiar coerciveness of ideas, that will methodically eliminate all seductions except for the purely intellectual. Once that state of mental readiness has been achieved (something one can only know for oneself, Descartes would insist), the mind's *subjective* responses — its convictions — can be trusted. While Gassendi and other critics have complained of the lack of an "objective" test of ideas, Descartes, I propose, was up to something entirely different: He was offering a program of purification and training — for the liberation of *res cogitans* from the confusion and obscurity of its bodily swamp.

THE CARTESIAN WAY WITH DUALISM

Disdain for the body, the conception of it as an alien force and an impediment to the soul, is, of course, very old in our Greco-Christian traditions. Descartes was not the first philosopher to charge the body with responsibility for obscurity and confusion in our thinking. Rather, as Plato says in the *Phaedo*, " . . . it is characteristic of the philosopher to despise the body" (65). And, according to Plato, this disdain is well-founded: "A source of countless distractions by reason of the mere requirement of food, liable also to diseases which overtake and impede us in the pursuit of truth: [the body] fills us full of loves, and lusts, and fears, and fancies of all kinds, and endless foolery, and in very truth, as men say, takes away from us the power of thinking at all" (66c).

Descartes, then, was not the first philosopher to view the body with disdain. Platonic and neo-Platonic thought, and the Christian traditions that grew out of them, all exhibit such a strain. Nor was Descartes the first to view human existence as bifurcated into the realms of the physical and the spiritual, with the physical cast in the role of the alien and impure. For Plato, the body is often described via the imagery of separateness from the self: It is "fastened and glued" to me, "nailed" and "riveted" to me (83d). Images of the body-as-confinement from which the soul struggles to escape — "prison," "cage" — abound in Plato, as they do in Descartes. For Plato, as for Augustine later, the body is the locus of all that which threatens our attempts at control. It overtakes, it overwhelms, it erupts and disrupts. This situation becomes an incitement to battle the unruly forces of the body. Although less methodically than Descartes, Plato provides instruction on how to gain control over the body, how to achieve intellectual independence from the lure of its illusions and become impervious to its distractions. A central theme of the *Phaedo*, in fact, is the philosopher's training in developing such independence from the body.

But while dualism runs deep in our traditions, it is only with Descartes that body and mind are *defined* in terms of mutual exclusivity. For Plato (and Aristotle), the living body is permeated with soul, which can only depart the body at death. For Descartes, on the other hand, soul and body become two distinct substances. The body is pure *res extensa* — unconscious, extended stuff, brute materiality. "Every kind of thought which exists in us," he says in the *Passions of the Soul*, "belongs to the soul" (HR, I, 332). The soul, on the other hand, is pure *res cogitans* — mental, incorporeal, without location, *bodyless*: " . . . in its nature entirely independent of body, and not in any way derived from the power of matter" (*Discourse*, HR, I, 118).

The mutual exclusivity of mind and body has important consequences. Plato's and Aristotle's view that "soul" is a principle of life is one which Descartes takes great pains to refute in the *Passions of the Soul*. For Descartes, rather, the "life" of the body is a matter of purely mechanical functioning.

> [W]e may judge that the body of a living man differs from that of a dead man just as does a watch or other automaton (i.e., a machine that moves of itself), when it is wound up and contains in itself the corporeal principle of those movements for which it is designated along with all that is requisite for its action, from the same watch or other machine when it is broken and when the principle of its movement ceases to act (HR, I, 333).

While the body is thus likened to a machine, the mind (having been conceptually purified of all material "contamination") is defined by precisely and only those qualities which the human being shares with God: freedom, will, consciousness. For Descartes there is no ambiguity or complexity here. The body is excluded from all participation, all connection with God; the soul alone represents the godliness and the goodness of the human being.

In Plato and Aristotle, the lines simply cannot be drawn in so stark a fashion. In the *Symposium*, we should remember, the love of the body is the first, and necessary, step on the spiritual ladder which leads to the glimpsing of the eternal form of beauty. For the Greek philosophers, the body is not simply an impediment to knowledge; it may also function as a spur to spiritual growth. Its passions may motivate the quest for knowledge and beauty. Moreover, since soul is inseparable from body except at death, any human aspirations to intellectual "purity" during one's lifetime are merely wishful fantasy. "While in company with the body the soul cannot have pure knowledge." Plato unequivocally declares in the *Phaedo*..

For the Greeks, then, there are definite limits to the human intellect. For Descartes, on the other hand, epistemological hubris knows few bounds.[10] The dream of purity is realizable during one's lifetime. For, given the right method, one can transcend the body. This is, of course, what Descartes believed himself to have accomplished in the *Meditations*. Addressing Gassendi as "O flesh!" he describes himself as "a mind so far withdrawn from corporeal things that it does not even know that anyone has existed before it" (HR, II, 214).

That such a radical program of mental purification is so central to the Cartesian epistemological program is not surprising. For, the body is not only the organ of the deceptive senses, and the site of disruption and "commotion" in the heart, blood, and animal spirits. It is also the most brute, pressing and ubiquitous reminder of how *located* and perspectival our experience and thought is, how bounded in time and space. "Birth, the past, contingency, the necessity of a point of view . . . such is the body," says Sartre. The Cartesian knower, the other hand, being without a body, not only has "no need of any place" (*Discourse*, HR, I, p. 101) but actually *is* "no place." He[11] therefore cannot "grasp" the universe — which would demand a place "outside" the whole. But, assured of his own transparency, he can relate with absolute neutrality to the objects he surveys, unfettered by the perspectival nature of embodied vision. He has become, quite literally, "*objective.*"

Not only, in this way, is the spectre of "subjectivity" laid to rest, but the very impersonality of the post-Copernican universe is turned to human advantage. For impersonality has become the mark of the truth of the known. Resistant to human will, immune to every effort of the knower to make it what *he* would have it be rather than what is "is," purified of all "inessential" spiritual associations and connections with the rest of the universe, the clear and distinct idea is both compensation for and conqueror of the cold, new world.

Chapter Six

THE CARTESIAN MASCULINIZATION OF THOUGHT AND THE SEVENTEENTH-CENTURY FLIGHT FROM THE FEMININE

> [I]f a kind of Cartesian ideal were ever completely fulfilled, i.e., if the whole of nature were only what can be explained in terms of mathematical relationships — then we would look at the world with that fearful sense of alienation, with that utter loss of reality with which a future schizophrenic child looks at his mother. A machine cannot give birth.
>
> Karl Stern, *The Flight From Woman*

PHILOSOPHICAL RECONSTRUCTION, ANXIETY AND FLIGHT

If the transition from Middle Ages to early modernity can be looked on as a kind of protracted birth, from which the human being emerges as a decisively separate entity, no longer continuous with the universe with which it had once shared a soul, so the possibility of objectivity, strikingly, is conceived by Descartes as a kind of *rebirth*, on one's own terms, this time.

We are all familiar with the dominant Cartesian themes of starting anew, alone, without influence from the past or other people, with the guidance of reason alone. The product of our original and actual birth, childhood, being ruled by the body, is the source of most obscurity and confusion in our thinking. As Descartes says in the *Discourse*, "since we have all been children before being men . . . it is almost impossible that our judgements should be so excellent or solid as they would have been had we had complete use of our reason since our birth, and had we been guided by its means alone" (HR, I, 88). The specific origins of obscurity in our thinking are, as we have seen, the appetites, the influence of our teachers, and the "preju- dices" of childhood. Those "prejudices" all have a common form: the inability, due to our infantile "immersion" in the body, to distinguish prop- erly between subject and object. The purification of the relation between knower and known requires the repudiation of childhood, a theme which was not uncommon at the time. The ideology of childhood as a time of "innocence," and the child as an epistemological *tabula rasa*, had yet to become popular (Aries, 100–133). Rather, childhood was commonly associated, as Descartes associated it, with sensuality, animality, and the mystifications of the body.[1]

For Descartes, happily, the state of childhood *can* be revoked, through a deliberate and methodical reversal of all the prejudices acquired within it, and a beginning anew with reason as one's only parent. This is precisely what the *Meditations* attempts to do. The mind is emptied of all that it has been taught. The body of infancy, preoccupied with appetite and sense- experience, is transcended. The clear and distinct ideas are released from their obscuring material prison. The end-result is a philosophical reconstruc- tion which secures all the boundaries which, in childhood (and at the start of the *Meditations*) are so fragile: between the "inner" and the "outer," bet- ween the subjective and the objective, between self and world.

It is crucial to recall here that what for Descartes is conceived as epistemological threat — "subjectivity," or the blurring of boundaries between self and world — was not conceived as such by the medievals. Rather, the medieval sense of relatedness to the world, as we know from its art, literature, and philosophy, had not depended on "objectivity" but on continuity between the human and physical realms, on the interpenetra- tions, through meanings, of self and world. But *locatedness* in space and time, by Descartes's era, had inexorably come to the forefront of human exper- ience, and the continuities and interpenetrations which had once been a source of intellectual and spiritual satisfaction now presented themselves as "distortions" caused by personal attachment and "perspective." Objectivity, not meaning, became the issue, and "so long as the human being is embed- ded in nature and united with it, objectivity is impossible" (Stern, 76). By the time of Kant, this "condition" for knowledge — the separation of knower and known — is philosophically apprehended. Human intelligence, Kant discovers, is *founded* on the distinction between subject and object. The condition of *having* an objective world, on the Kantian view, is to grasp phenomena as unified and connected by the embrace of a discrete consciousness, capable of representing to itself its own distinctness from the world it grasps. But what Kant here "discovers" (and what came to be regarded as a given in modern science and philosophy) was a while in the making. For Descartes, the separation of subject and object is a *project*, not a "foundation" to be discovered.

As we saw in the preceding essay, the Cartesian reconstruction has two interrelated dimensions. On the one hand, a new model of knowledge is conceived, in which the purity of the intellect is guaranteed through its ability to transcend the body. On the other hand, the ontological blueprint of the order of things is refashioned. The spiritual and the corporeal are now two distinct substances which share no qualities (other than being created), permit of interaction but no merging, and are each defined precisely in opposition to the other. *Res cogitans* is "a thinking and unextended thing"; *res extensa* is "an extended and unthinking thing" (I, 190). This mutual exclusion of *res cogitans* and *res extensa* made possible the conceptualization of complete intellectual independence from the body, *res extensa* of the human being and chief impediment to human objectivity. The dictotomy between the spiritual and the corporeal also established the utter diremption of the natural world from the realm of the human.[2] It now became inappropriate to speak, as the medievals had done, in anthropocentric terms about nature, which for Descartes is pure *res extensa*, "totally devoid of mind and thought." More important, it means that the values and significances of things in relation to the human realm must be understood as purely a reflection of how *we* feel about them, having nothing to do with their "objective" qualities.

"Thus," says Whitehead, in sardonic criticism of the "characteristic scientific philosophy" of the seventeenth century, "the poets are entirely mistaken. They should address their lyrics to themselves, and should turn them into odes of self-congratulation . . . Nature is a dull affair, soundless, scentless, colourless; merely the hurrying of material, endlessly, meaninglessly" (1925, p. 54). For the model of knowledge which results, neither bodily response (the sensual or the emotional) nor associational thinking, exploring the various personal or spiritual meanings the object has for us, can tell us anything about the object "itself." *It* can only be grasped, as Gillispie puts it, "by measurement rather than sympathy" (p. 42). Thus, the specter of infantile subjectivism is overcome by the possibility of a cool, impersonal, distanced cognitive relation to the world. At the same time, the nightmare landscape of the infinite universe has become the well-lighted laboratory of modern science and philosophy.

The conversion of nightmare into positive vision is characteristic of Descartes. Within the narrative framework of the *Meditations*, "dreamers, demons, and madmen" are exorcised, the crazily fragmented "enchanted glass" of the mind (as Bacon called it) is transformed into the "mirror of nature," the true reflector of things. But such transformations, as Descartes's determinedly upbeat interpretation of his own famous nightmare suggests, may be grounded in *defense* — in the suppression of anxiety, uncertainty, and dread. Certainly, anxiety infuses the *Meditations*, as I have argued through my reading of the text. I have tried, too, to show that Cartesian anxiety was a *cultural* anxiety, arising from discoveries, inventions, and events which were major and disorienting.

That disorientation, I have suggested, is given psychocultural coherence via a "story" of *parturition* from the organic universe of the Middle Ages and Renaissance, out of which emerged the modern categories of "self," "locatedness," and "innerness." This parturition was initially experienced as *loss*, that is, as estrangement, and the opening up of a chasm between self and nature. Epistemologically, that estrangement expresses itself in a renewal of scepticism, and in an unprecedented anxiety over the possibility of reaching the world as "it" is. Spiritually, it expresses itself in anxiety over the *enclosedness* of the individual self, the isolating uniqueness of each individual allotment in time and space, and the arbitrary, incomprehensible nature of that allotment by an alien, indifferent universe. We may speak here, meaningfully, of a *cultural* "separation anxiety."

The particular genius of Descartes was to have philosophically transformed what was first experienced as estrangement and loss — the sundering of the organic ties between the person and world — into a requirement for the growth of human knowledge and progress. And at this point, we are in a better position to flesh out the mechanism of *defense* involved here. Cartesian objectivism and mechanism, I will propose, should be understood as a *reaction-formation* — a denial of the "separation anxiety" described above, facilitated by an aggressive intellectual *flight* from the female cosmos and "feminine" orientation towards the world. That orientation (described so far in this study in the gender-neutral terminology of "participating consciousness") had still played a formidable role in medieval and Renaissance thought and culture. In the seventeenth century, it was decisively purged from the dominant intellectual culture, through the Cartesian "re-birthing" and restructuring of knowledge and world as *masculine*.

I will begin by exploring the mechanist flight from the female cosmos (which Carolyn Merchant has called "The Death of Nature"). Then, I will focus on the specifically epistemological expression of the seventeenth-century flight from the feminine: "the Cartesian masculinization of thought." Both the mechanist reconstruction of the world and the objectivist reconstruction of knowledge will then be examined as embodying a common psychological structure: a fantasy of "re-birthing" self and world, brought into play by the disintegration of the organic, female cosmos of the Middle Ages and Renaissance. This philosophical fantasy will be situated within the general context of seventeenth-century attitudes toward female generativity, as chronicled by a number of feminist authors. Finally, the relevance of these ideas to current discussions about gender and rationality, and to current reassessments of Cartesianism, will be considered in a concluding section of this chapter.

THE DEATH OF NATURE AND THE MASCULINIZATION OF THOUGHT

Discussion of "masculinity" and "femininity" is a new motif in this study. Yet gender has played an implicit role all along. For the medieval cosmos whose destruction gave birth to the modern sensibility was a *mother*-cosmos, and the soul which Descartes drained from the natural world was a *female* soul. Carolyn Merchant, whose ground-breaking interdisciplinary study, *The Death of Nature*, chronicles the changing imagery of nature in this period, describes the "organic cosmology" which mechanism overthrew:

> Minerals and metals ripened in the uterus of the Earth Mother, mines were compared to her vagina, and metallurgy was the human hastening of the living metal in the artificial womb of the furnace . . . Miners offered propitiation to the deities of the soil, performed ceremonial sacrifices . . . sexual abstinence, fasting, before violating the sacredness of the living earth by sinking a mine (p. 4).

The notion of the natural world as *mothered* has sources, for the Western tradition, in both Plato and Aristotle. In Plato's *Timeaus*, the formless "receptacle" or "nurse" provides the substratum of all determinate materiality. (As noted in essay four, it is also referred to as "space" — *chora* — in the dialogue.) The "receptacle" is likened to a mother because of its receptivity to impression; the father is the "source or spring" — the eternal forms which "enter" and "stir and inform her." The child is the determinate nature which is formed through their union: the *body* of nature (51).

In this account, the earth is not a mother, but is itself a child of the union of "nurse" and forms. The notion that the earth *itself* mothers things, for example, metals and minerals, required the inspiration of the Aristotelian theory of animal reproduction. In that theory, the female provides not only matter as "substratum," but matter as sensible "stuff": the *catamenia*, or menstral material, which is "worked upon" and shaped by the "effective and active" element, the semen of the male (729a–729b). In the fifteenth and sixteenth centuries, this account of animal generation was "projected" onto the cosmos. A "stock description" of biological generation in nature was the marriage of heaven and earth, and the impregnation of the (female) earth by the dew and rain created by the movements of the (masculine) celestial heavens (Merchant, 16).

The female element here is *natura naturata*, of course — passive rather than creative nature. But passivity here connotes *receptivity* rather than inertness; only a living, breathing earth can be impregnated. And indeed, for Plato most explicitly, the world *has* a soul — a female soul — which permeates the corporeal body of the universe. In the seventeenth century, as Merchant argues, that female world-soul died — or more precisely, was *murdered* — by the mechanist re-visioning of nature.

This re-visioning of the universe as a *machine* — most often, a clockwork — was not the work of philosophers alone. Astronomy and anatomy had already changed the dominant picture of the movements of the heavens and the processes of the body by the time the *Meditations* were written. But it was philosophy, and Descartes in particular, that provided the cosmology that integrated these discoveries into a consistent and unified view of nature. By Descartes's brilliant stroke, nature became *defined* by its lack of affiliation with divinity, with spirit. All that which is God-like or spiritual — freedom, will, and sentience — belong entirely and exclusively to *res cogitans*. All else — the earth, the heavens, animals, the human body — is merely mechanically interacting matter.

The seventeenth century saw the death, too, of another sort of "feminine principle" — that cluster of epistemological values, often associated with feminine consciousness,[3] and which apparently played a large and respected role in hermetic philosophy and, it might be argued, in the prescientific orientation toward the world in general. If the key terms in the Cartesian hierarchy of epistemological values are clarity and distinctness — qualities which mark each object off from the other and from the knower — the key term in this alternative scheme of values might be designated (following Gillispie's contrast here) as *sympathy*. "Sympathetic" understanding of the object is that which understands it through "union" with it (Stern, 42–43), or, as James Hillman describes it, though "merging with" or "marrying" it.

To merge with or marry that which is to be known means, for Hillman, "letting interior movement replace clarity, interior closeness replace objectivity" (*The Myth of Analysis*, 293). It means granting personal or intuitive response a positive epistemological value, even (perhaps especially) when such response is contradictory or fragmented. "Sympathetic" thinking, Marcuse suggests, is the only mode which truly respects the object, that is, which allows the variety of its meanings to unfold without coercion or too-focused interrogation (p. 74).

Barfield's and Berman's discussions of medieval "participating consciousness," Bergson's notion of "intellectual sympathy," Jasper's "causality from within," all contain elements of what I have here called "sympathetic thinking." The deepest understanding of that which is to be known comes, each argues, not from analysis of parts but from "placing oneself within" the full being of an object, as Bergson puts it, (at which point it ceases to be an "object" in the usual sense) and allowing *it* to speak.

An emphasis on the knower's *passivity* is shared by this ideal of knowledge and the Cartesian ideal. But whereas passivity for Descartes (and for Bacon) meant yielding to the authority of the object's "own" nature, for sympathetic thinking, the objective and subjective *merge*, participate in the creation of meaning. The most inspired and articulate contemporary advocates of what I am here calling "sympathetic thinking" are Carol Gilligan (1982) and Evelyn Fox Keller (1985), each of whom speaks forcefully to the need for integration of such thinking into our dominant conceptions of rationality. This does not mean a rejection, but a *re-visioning* of "objectivity." Keller's conception of "dynamic objectivity" is especially relevant here:

> Dynamic objectivity is . . . a pursuit of knowledge that makes use of subjective experience . . . in the interests of a more effective objectivity. Premised on continuity, it recognizes difference between self and other as an opportunity for a deeper and more articulated kinship. The struggle to disentangle self from other is itself a source of insight — potentially into the nature of both self and other. It is a principle means for divining what Poincaré calls "hidden harmonies and relations." To this end, the scientist employs a form of attention to the natural world that is like one's ideal attention to the human world: it is a form of love (p. 117).

In contrast to the conception of "dynamic objectivity," Descartes's program for the purification of the understanding, as we have seen, has as its ideal the rendering *impossible* of any such continuity between subject and object. The scientific mind must be cleansed of all its "sympathies" toward the objects it tries to understand. It must cultivate absolute *detachment*. Recognizing the centrality of such ideals to modern science has led writers like Sandra Harding to characterize modern science in terms of a "super-masculinization of rational thought."[4] Similarly, Karl Stern has said that "[what] we encounter in Cartesian rationalism is the pure masculinization of thought" (p. 104). The notion that modern science crystallizes masculinist modes of thinking is a theme, too, in the work of James Hillman; "The specific consciousness we call scientific, Western and modern," says Hillman, "is the long sharpened tool of the masculine mind that has discarded parts of its own substance, calling it 'Eve,' 'female,' and 'inferior'" (*The Myth of Analysis*, 250). Evelyn Fox Keller's *Reflections On Gender and Science* systematically explores various perspectives (including developmental perspectives) on the connection between masculinity and modern science.

It must be stressed that descriptions of modern science as a "masculinization of thought" refer to what these authors view as characteristic cognitive and theoretical biases of male-dominated science, *not* the fact of that male dominance itself, or science's attitudes toward women. Science has, of course, a long history of discrimination against women, insisting that women cannot measure up to the rigor, persistence, or clarity that science requires. It also has its share of explicitly misogynist doctrine, as does its ancient forefathers, Aristotle and Galen. But the most interesting contemporary discussions of the "masculinist" nature of modern science describe a different, though related, aspect of its "masculinism": a characteristic cognitive style, an epistemological stance which is required of men *and* women working in the sciences today. In the words of Evelyn Fox Keller:

> The scientific mind is set apart from what is to be known, i.e., from nature, and its autonomy is guaranteed . . . by setting apart its modes of knowing from those in which the dichotomy is threatened. In this process, the characterization of both the scientific mind and its modes of access to knowledge as masculine is indeed significant. Masculine here connotes, as it so often does, autonomy, separation, and distance . . . a radical rejection of any commingling of subject and object (p. 79).

It is in this sense that the dominant scientific and philosophic culture of the seventeenth century indeed inaugurated "a truly masculine birth of time," as Francis Bacon had proclaimed it (Farrington). Similarly and strikingly, Henry Oldenberg, secretary of the Royal Society, asserted in 1664 that the business of that society was to raise "a masculine philosophy" (Easlea, 152). In her penetrating and imaginative study of sexual metaphors in the history of epistemology, Keller pays very serious attention to such historical associations of gender and "cognitive style," which we might have thought to belong to a peculiarly contemporary mentality, but which in fact crop up frequently in Royal Society debates. As Keller reads them, the controversies between Bacon and Paracelsus become an explicit contest between masculine and feminine principles: head versus heart, domination over versus merging with the object, purified versus erotic orientation toward knowledge, and so forth (43–65). Bacon's own deepest attitudes, Keller suggests, were more complicated and ambivalent than his oft-reproduced and notorious images of male seduction, penetration, and rape of nature may indicate. But what emerges with clarity, despite any subtleties in the attitudes of individual thinkers, is that the notion of science as "masculine" is hardly a twentieth-century invention or feminist fantasy. The founders of modern science consciously and explicitly proclaimed the "masculinity" of science as inaugurating a new era. And they associated that masculinity with a cleaner, purer, more objective and more disciplined epistemological relation to the world.

The emergence of such associations, in an era which lacked our heightened modern consciousness of gender as an issue, is remarkable. They suggest that the contemporary notion that thought *became* "super-masculinized" at a certain point in time is not merely, as some might argue, a new, fashionable way of labelling and condemning the seventeenth-century objectivist turn — a turn, many would say, which has already been adequately described, criticized, and laid to rest by Whitehead, Heidegger, and, more recently, Richard Rorty. Bacon's metaphor, rather, urges us in the direction of confronting a profound "flight from the feminine" at the heart of both Cartesian rationalism and Baconian empiricism. To appreciate the dimensions of that "flight," however, necessitates a return to the insights of developmental psychology.

THE CARTESIAN "REBIRTH" AND THE "FATHER OF ONESELF" FANTASY

> Descartes envisages for himself a kind of rebirth. Intellectual salvation comes only to the twice-born.— Frankfurt, *Demons, Dreamers, and Madmen*

Psychoanalytic theory urges us to examine that which we actively repudiate for the shadow of a loss we mourn. Freud, in *Beyond the Pleasure Principle*, tells the story of an eighteen-month-old boy — an obedient, orderly little boy, as Freud describes him — who, although "greatly attached to his mother," never cried when she left him for a few hours.

This good little boy, however, had an occasional disturbing habit of taking any small objects he could get hold of and throwing them away from him into a corner, under the bed, and so on, so that hunting for his toys and picking them up was often quite a business. As he did this he gave vent to a loud, long-drawn-out 'o-o-o-o', accompanied by an expression of interest and satisfaction. His mother and the writer of the present account were agreed in thinking that this was not a mere interjection but represented the German word '*fort*' ('gone'). I eventually realized that it was a game and that the only use he made of any of his toys was to play 'gone' with them . . . [T]he complete game [was] disappearance and return . . . The interpretation . . . became obvious. It was related to the child's great cultural achievement — the instinctual renunciation (that is, the renunciation of instinctual satisfaction) which he had made in allowing his mother to go away without protesting. He compensated himself for this, as it were, by himself staging the disappearance and return of the objects within his reach . . . Throwing away the object so that it was 'gone' might satisfy an impulse of the child's, which was suppressed in his actual life, to revenge himself on his mother for going away from him. In that case it would have a defiant meaning: 'All right, then, go away! I don't need you. I'm sending you away myself' (33–35).

The "fort-da" game and Freud's interpretation of it places the Cartesian facility for transforming anxiety into confidence, loss into mastery, in a striking new perspective. Within the context of the cultural separation anxiety described in this study, Descartes's masculine "rebirthing" of the world and self as decisively separate appears, not merely as the articulation of a positive new epistemological ideal, but as a reaction-formation to the loss of "being-one-with-the-world" brought about by the disintegration of the organic, centered, female cosmos of the Middle Ages and Renaissance. The Cartesian reconstruction of the world is a "fort-da" game — a defiant gesture of independence from the female cosmos, a gesture which is at the same time compensation for a profound loss.

Let us explore the interpretation proposed above in more detail, turning again to developmental theory for insight. The project of growing up is to one degree or another (depending on culture and child-raising practice) a project of *separation*, of learning to deal with the fact that mother and child are no longer one and that gratification is not always available. Social and personal strategies for the child's accomplishing this are varied; every culture no doubt has its own modes of facilitating the separation of mother and child, to the degree that such separation is required by the culture. Psychoanalytic theory has focused on *internal* mechanisms, describing the different responses — longing, mourning, denial — that the child may have to separation. The mechanism of *denial* is of particular interest for my purposes. Although the dream of total union can persist throughout life, another, contradictory project may be conceived, pychoanalytic thinkers have suggested, centered around the denial of any longing for the lost maternal union. Instead, the child seeks mastery over the frustrations of separation and lack of gratification through an assertion of self against the mother and all that she represents and a rejection of all dependency on her. In this way, the pain of separateness is assuaged, paradoxically, by an even more definitive separation — but one that is *chosen* this time and aggressively pursued. It is therefore experienced as autonomy rather than helplessness in the fact of the discontinuity between self and mother.

One mode of such self-assertion is through the fantasy of becoming the parent of oneself, of "rebirthing" the self, playing the role of active parental figure rather than passive, helpless child. Such a notion of "rebirthing" or "reparenting" the self figures in both Freudian and object-relations frameworks. Building on Winnicott's concept of the "transitional object" (a blanket, toy, or stuffed animal which eases the child's accommodation to and ultimate mastery over the process of separation from the mother), Ross argues that such objects function, symbolically, as the child himself. In cuddling and scolding the object, the child is actually playing at self-parenting, at being his own baby. Such self-parenting allows the child to feel less precariously at the mercy of the mother, more in control of his or her own destiny (1977).

Working from a more Freudian framework, Norman O. Brown reinterprets the Oedipal desire to "sexually" possess the mother as a fantasy of "beoming the father of oneself" (rather than the helpless child of the mother) (p. 127). Sexual activity here (or rather, the fantasy of it) becomes a means of denying the actual passivity of having been born from that original state of union into "a body of limited powers, and at a time and place [one] never chose" (deBeauvoir, 146), at the mercy of the now-alien will of the mother. The mother is still "other," but she is an other whose power has been harnessed by the will of the child. The pain of separateness is thus compensated for by the peculiar advantages of separateness: the possibility of mastery and control over that person on whom one is dependent. Melanie Klein (writing in 1928, much earlier than Brown) emphasizes the aggressive, destructive, envious impulses which may be directed against parts of the mother's body — particularly against the breasts and reproductive organs — in the child's effort to achieve such control (pp. 98–111).

Certainly, the famous Baconian imagery of sexual assault and aggressive overpowering of a willful and unruly female nature (she must "be taken by the forelock" and "neither ought a man to make scruple of entering and penetrating these holes and corners," etc.[5]) makes new psychocultural sense in the context of these ideas. More subtly, the Cartesian project of starting anew through the revocation of one's actual childhood (during which one was "immersed" in body and nature) and the (re)creation of a world in which absolute separateness (both epistemological and ontological) from body and nature are keys to control rather than sources of anxiety can now be seen as a "father of oneself" fantasy on a highly symbolic, but profound, plane.[6] The sundering of the organic ties between person and nature — originally experienced, as we have seen, as epistemological estrangement, as the opening up of a chasm between self and world — is reenacted, *this* time with the human being as the engineer and architect of the separation. Through the Cartesian "rebirth," a new "masculine" theory of knowledge is delivered, in which detachment from nature acquires a positive epistemological value. And a new *world* is reconstructed, one in which all generativity and creativity fall to God, the spiritual father, rather than to the female "flesh" of the world. With the same masterful stroke — the mutual opposition of the spiritual and the corporeal — the formerly female earth becomes inert matter and the objectivity of science is insured.

"She" becomes "it" — and "it" can be understood and controlled. Not through "sympathy," of course, but by virtue of the very *object*-ivity of the "it." At the same time, the "wound" of separateness is healed through the *denial* that there ever "was" any union: For the mechanists, unlike Donne, the female world-soul did not die; rather the world *is* dead. There is nothing to mourn, nothing to lament. Indeed, the "new" epistemological anxiety is evoked, not over loss, but by the "memory" or suggestion of *union*; "sympathetic," associational, or bodily response obscures objectivity, feeling for nature muddies the clear lake of the mind. The "otherness" of nature is now what allows it to be known.

THE SEVENTEENTH-CENTURY FLIGHT FROM THE FEMININE

The philosophical "murder" of the living female earth, explored in the preceding section as a reaction-formation to the dissolution of the medieval self-world unity, must be placed in the context of other issues in the gender politics of the sixteenth and seventeenth centuries. Thanks to the historical research of such writers as Carolyn Merchant, Brian Easlea, Barbara Ehrenreich, Dierdre English, and Adrienne Rich, we have been enabled to recognize the years between 1550 and 1650 as a particularly gynophobic century. What has been especially brought to light is what now appears as a virtual obsession with the untamed natural power of female generativity, and a dedication to bringing it under forceful cultural control.

Nightmare fantasies of female power over reproduction and birth run throughout the era. Kramer and Sprenger's *Malleus Maleficarum*, the official witch-hunter's handbook, accuses "witches" of every imaginable natural and supernatural crime involving conception and birth. The failure of crops and miscarriages were attributed to witches, and they are accused both of "inclining men to passion" and of causing impotence, of obstructing fertility in both men and women, of removing the penises of men, or procuring abortion, and of offering newborns to the devil (Lederer, 209).

Such fantasies were not limited to a fanatic fringe. Among the scientific set, we find the image of the witch, the willful, wanton virago, projected onto generative nature, whose scientific exploration, as Merchant points out, is metaphorically likened to a witch trial (169–170). The "secrets" of nature are imagined as deliberately and slyly "concealed" from the scientist (Easlea, 214). Matter, which in the *Timeaus* is passively receptive to the ordering and shaping masculine forms, now becomes, for Bacon, a "common harlot" with "an appetite and inclination to dissolve the world and fall back into the old chaos" and who must therefore be "restrained and kept in order" (Merchant 171). The womb of nature, too, (and this is striking, in connection with Melanie Klein) is no longer the beneficent mother but rather the *hoarder* of precious metals and minerals, which must be "searched" and "spied out" (Merchant, 169–70).

There were the witchhunts themselves, which, aided more politely by the gradual male takeover of birthing, and healing in general, virtually purged the healing arts of female midwives.[7] The resulting changes in obstetrics, which rendered women passive and dependent in the process of birth, came to identify birth, as Bacon identified nature itself, with the potentiality of disorder and the need for forceful male control.[8] So, too, in the seventeenth century, female sexuality was seen as voracious and insatiable, and a principle motivation behind witchcraft, which offered the capacious "mouth of the womb" the opportunity to copulate with the devil.[9]

The ideology of the voracious, insatiable female may not be unique to the sixteenth and seventeenth centuries. But it is not historically ubiquitous. By the second half of the nineteenth century, medical science had declared women to be naturally passive and "not much troubled by sexual feeling of any kind" (Vicinus, 82). Peter Gay suggests that this medical fantasy was a reaction-formation to that era's "pervasive sense of manhood in danger" (p.

93), brought about by its own particular social disruptions in gender relations and the family. I would suggest, along similar lines, that key changes
in the seventeenth-century scientific theory of reproduction functioned in
much the same way, although in reaction to different threats and
disruptions.

Generativity, not sexuality, is the focus of the seventeenth century's
fantasies of female passivity. Mechanist reproductive theory ("happily," as
Brian Easlea sarcastically puts it) made it "no longer necessary to refer to any
women at all" in its "scientific" descriptions of conception and gestation
(Easlea, 49). Denied even her limited, traditional Aristotelian role of supplying the (living) menstrual material (which, shaped by the individuating male
"form" results in the fetus), the woman becomes instead the mere *container*
for the temporary housing and incubation of already-formed human beings,
originally placed in Adam's semen by God, and parcelled out, over the ages,
to all his male descendents.[10] The specifics of mechanistic reproductive
theory are a microcosmic recapitulation of the mechanistic vision itself,
where God the father is the sole creative, formative principle in the cosmos.
We know, from what now must be seen as almost paradigmatic examples of
the power of belief over perception, that tiny horses and men were actually
"seen" by mechanist scientists examining sperm under their microscopes.

All this is only to scratch the surface of a literature that has become quite
extensive over the last decade. Even this brief survey, however, yields striking
parallels. The mechanization of nature, we see, theoretically "quieted" the
"common harlot" of matter (and sanctioned nature's exploitation) as effectively as Baconian experimental philosophy did so practically. Mechanistic
reproductive theory successfully eliminated any active, generative role for the
female in the processes of conception and gestation. And *actual* control over
reproduction and birth was wrested away from women by the witch-hunters
and the male medical establishment. Something, it seems, had come to be
felt as all too powerful and in need of taming.

What can account for this upsurge of fear of female generativity? No
doubt many factors — economic, political, and institutional — are crucial.
But I would suggest that the themes of "parturition" and "separation
anxiety" discussed in this study can provide an illuminative psychocultural
framework within which to situate seventeenth-century gynophobia.

The culture in question, in the wake of the dissolution of the medieval
intellectual and imaginative system, had lost a world in which the human
being could feel nourished by the sense of oneness, of continuity between
all things. The new, infinite universe was an indifferent home, an "alien will,"

and the sense of separateness from her was acute. Not only was she "other," but she seemed a perverse and uncontrollable other. During the years 1550–1650, a century that had brought the worst food crisis in history, violent wars, plague, and devastating poverty, the Baconian imagery of nature as an unruly and malevolent virago was no paranoid fantasy. More important, the cruelty of the world could no longer be made palatable by the old medieval sense of organic justice — that is, justice on the level of the workings of a whole with which one's identity merged and which, while perhaps not fully comprehensible, was nonetheless to be trusted. Now there is no organic unity, but only "I" and "She" — an unpredictable and seemingly arbitrary "She," whose actions cannot be understood in any of the old "sympathetic" ways.

"She" is *Other.* And "otherness" itself becomes dreadful — particularly the otherness of the female, whose powers have always been mysterious to men, and evocative of the mystery of existence itself. Like the infinite universe, which threatens to swallow the individual "like a speck," the female, with her strange rhythms, long acknowledged to have their chief affinities with the rhythms of the natural (now alien) world, becomes a reminder of how much lies outside the grasp of man.

"The quintessential incarnation" of that which appears to man as "mysterious, powerful and not himself," as Dorothy Dinnerstein says, is "the woman's fertile body" (p. 125). Certainly, the mother's body holds these meanings for the infant, according to Klein. If Dorothy Dinnerstein is right, women (particularly the woman-as-mother, the original "representative" of the natural world, and virtually indistinguishable from it for the human infant) are always likely targets for all later adult rage against nature.[11] Supporting Dinnerstein's highly theoretical account are the anthropologist Peggy Reeves Sanday's cross-cultural findings that in periods of cultural disruption and environmental stress, male social dominance — particularly over female fertility — tends to be at its most extreme (172–84). In the seventeenth century, with the universe appearing to man more decisively "not-himself" than ever before, more capricious and more devastating in her capacity for disorder, both the mystery of the universe and the mystery of the female require a more definitive "solution" than had been demanded by the organic world view.[12]

The project that fell to both empirical science and "rationalism" was to tame the female universe. Empirical science did this through aggressive assault and violation of her "secrets." Rationalism, as we have seen, tamed the female universe through the philosophical neutralization of her vitality.

The barrenness of matter correlatively insured the revitalization of human hope of conquering nature (through knowledge, in this case, rather than through force). The mystery of the female, however, could not be bent to man's control simply through philosophical means. More direct and concrete means of "neutralization" were required for that project. It is within this context that witch-hunting and the male medical takeover of the processes of reproduction and birth, whatever their social and political causes, can be seen to have a profound psychocultural dimension as well.

The Contemporary Revaluation of the Feminine

My next focus will be on the recent scholarly emergence and revaluation of epistemological and ethical perspectives "in a different voice." That voice, which classical as well as contemporary writers identify as feminine (as, e.g., in the work of Carol Gilligan, Sarah Ruddick, and Nancy Chodorow), claims a natural foundation for knowledge, not in detachment and distance, but in what I have called "sympathy": in closeness, connectedness, and empathy. It finds the failure of connection (rather than the blurring of boundaries) as the principle cause of breakdown in understanding.

In the seventeenth century, when Paracelsus articulated the alchemical conception of knowledge as a merger of mind and nature, the "female" nature of this ideal operated for him as a metaphor, as did Bacon's contrasting ideal of a virile, "masculine" science. In the second half of our own more sociologically oriented century, women themselves — not some abstract "feminine principle" — have been identified as cultural bearers of the alternative, "sympathetic" scheme of values. The research of Chodorow and Gilligan, in particular, has suggested that men and women (growing up within a particular cultural framework, it needs emphasizing) *do* appear to experience and conceptualize events differently, the key differences centering around different conceptions of the self/world, self/other relation.

> Girls emerge . . . with a basis for "empathy" built into their primary defini-
> tion of self in a way that boys do not. Girls emerge with a stronger basis for
> experiencing another's needs or feelings as one's own (or thinking that one
> is so experiencing another's needs or feelings) . . . girls come to experience
> themselves as less differentiated than boys, more continuous with and related
> to the external object-world and as differently oriented to their inner object-
> world as well (Chodorow, 167).

Carol Gilligan has described how these developmental differences result, in men and women, in differing valuations of attachment and autonomy, and correspondingly different conceptions of morality.

The association of cognitive style with gender is in itself nothing new. We find it in ancient mythology, in archetypal psychology, in philosophical and scientific writings, and in a host of enduring popular stereotypes about men and women (for example, that women are more "intuitive," men are more "logical," etc.) In the second half of the nineteenth century, the celebration of a distinctively female moral sensibility was widely held by both feminists and sexual conservatives. What *is* new in the recent feminist exploration of gender and cognitive style is a (characteristically modern) emphasis on gender as a social construction, rather than a biological or ontological given. If men and women think differently, it is argued, that is not because the sexes inevitably embody timeless "male" and "female" principles of existence, but because the sexes have been brought up differently, develop different social abilities, have occupied very different power positions in most cultures. Using a psychoanalytic framework, Nancy Chodorow explores the origins of these differences in the differing degrees of individuation from the mother demanded of boys and girls in infancy.[13]

An appreciation of the *historical* nature of the masculine model of knowledge to which the feminine "different voice" is often contrasted helps to underscore that the embodiment of these gender-related perspectives in actual men and women is a cultural, not a biological phenomenon. There have been cultures in which (using *our* terms now, not necessarily theirs) men thought more "like women," and there may be a time in the future when they do so again. In our own time, many women may be coming to think more and more "like men." The conclusion is not, however, that any association of gender and cognitive style is a reactionary mythology with no explanatory value. For the sexual division of labor within the family in the modern era has indeed fairly consistently reproduced significant cognitive and emotional differences along sexual lines. The central importance of Chodorow's work has been to show that boys have tended to grow up learning to experience the world like Cartesians, while girls do not, *because* of developmental asymmetries resulting from female-dominated infant care, rather than biology, anatomy, or "nature."[14]

It is of crucial importance, however, that feminist scholars like Chodorow more explicitly and emphatically underscore the fact that they are describing elements of a social construction, characteristic of certain (though not all) forms of gender organization, and *not* the reified dualities of an "eternal feminine" and "essential masculine" nature. A great deal of current division among feminists rests on lack of clarity and understanding regarding this distinction. This is unfortunate, because the sociological emphasis and understanding of gender as a social construction is one crucial difference between the contemporary feminist revaluation of the "feminine" and the nineteenth-century doctrine of female moral superiority. Too often, recently, the two have been conflated.

A still more central difference between nineteenth-century and twentieth-century feminism is the contemporary feminist emphasis on the *insufficiency* of any ethics or rationality — "feminine" *or* "masculine" — that operates solely in one mode without drawing on the resources and perspective of the other.[15] The nineteenth-century celebration of a distinctively feminine sensibility and morality functioned in the *service* of pure masculinized thought, by insisting that each "sphere" remain distinct and undiluted by the other. This was, of course, precisely what the seventeenth-century masculinization of thought had accomplished — the exclusion of "feminine" modes of knowing, not from culture in general, but from the scientific and philosophical arenas, whose objectivity and purity needed to be guaranteed. Romanticizing "the feminine" within its "own" sphere is no alternative to Cartesianism, because it suggests that the feminine has a "proper" (domestic) place. Only in establishing the scientific and philosophical legitimacy of alternative modes of knowing in the *public* arena (rather than glorifying them in their own special sphere of family relations) do we present a real alternative to Cartesianism.

FEMINISM AND THE "RECESSIVE" STRAIN IN PHILOSOPHY

The Cartesian ideals are under attack in philosophy today, and philosophers who subscribe to those ideals, whether in their analytic or phenomenological embodiment, are on the defensive. Because philosophy has been so dominated by the Cartesian standpoint, the erosion of Cartesianism has been interpreted by some as signalling the "death of philosophy," and many of the current debates among philosophers are couched in those terms. If anything is dying, however, it is the intellectual rule of a particular model of knowledge and reality. Philosophers who grew up under that rule, and who were taught to identify philosophy *with* it, may experience the end of that rule as portending the "end of philosophy." But in fact, philosophy has always spoken in many voices (although they have seldom been heard by the Cartesian "cultural overseer"), some of which are being revived and renovated today. More significantly, alternative voices from those groups which philosophy has traditionally excluded are now offering the discipline the very means of its revitalization: the truths and values which it has suppressed from its dominant models. Those truths and values have been living underground, throughout the Cartesian reign, and are now emerging to make a claim on the culture.

This emergence cannot be adequately understood unless seen against the backdrop of the last several decades of social and political life. Philosophers may think that the widespread self-critique in which philosophy is currently engaged began with the publication of Richard Rorty's *Philosophy and the Mirror of Nature*. But (as Rorty would probably be the first to acknowledge), the impact of that work had much to do with its timely crystallization of historicist currents that had been gathering momentum since the 1960s. Those currents were themselves activated by the various "liberation" movements of that decade. There is a certain similarity here with the Renaissance, in the cultural reawakening to the multiplicity of possible human perspectives, and to the role of culture in shaping those perspectives. But in our era, the reawakening has occurred in the context of a recognition not merely of the undiscovered "other," but of the *suppressed* other. Women, people of color, and various ethnic and national groups have forced the culture into a critical reexamination not only of diversity (as occurred for Renaissance culture), but of the forces that *mask* diversity. That which appears as "dominant," by virtue of that very fact, comes to be suspect: It has a secret story to tell, in the alternative perspectives to which it has denied legitimacy, and in the historical and political circumstances of its own dominance.

Fueled by the historicist tradition in epistemology, psychoanalytic thought, *and* the political movement for women's rights, representation, and participation in cultural life, feminist ethics and epistemology now appears as one of the most vital forces in the development of post-Cartesian focus and paradigm. The feminist exposure of the gender biases in our dominant Western conceptions of science and ethics — the revelation that the history of their development, the lenses through which they see the world, their methods and priorities have been decisively shaped by the fact that it has been men who have determined their course — has come as a startling recognition to many contemporary male philosophers.[16] Inspired by the work of Gilligan, Chodorow, Harding, and Keller, feminist theory has been systematically questioning the historical identification of rationality, intelligence, "good thinking," and so forth, with the masculine modes of detachment and clarity, offering alternative models of fresher, more humane, and more hopeful approaches to science and ethics.[17]

It is not only in explicitly feminist writing that these phenomena are occuring. Many of the "new paradigms" being proposed in the recent spate of literature on modernity and modern science are grounded in sympathetic, participatory alternatives to Cartesianism. (See Berman and Capra, in particular.) In philosophy, a whole slew of reconsiderations of traditional epistemological "problems" such as relativism, perspectivism, the role of emotions and body in knowledge, the possibility of ultimate foundations, and so on, has brought the feminine perspective in through the back door, as it were. Without explicit commitment to feminism *or* "the feminine," philosophers are nontheless participating in a (long overdue) philosophical acknowledgement of the limitations of the masculine Cartesian model, and are recognizing how tightly it has held most modern philosophy in its grip.

This is not to say that detachment, clarity, and precision will cease to have enormous value in the process of understanding. Rather, our culture needs to reconceive the status of what Descartes assigned to the shadows. Such reevaluation has been a constant, although "recessive" strain in the history of philosophy since Descartes. Leibniz's declaration that each monad is its *own* "mirror" of the universe, Hume's insistence that "reason is and ought to be the slave of the passions," and, perhaps most importantly, Kant's revelation that objectivity itself is the result of human structuring, opened various doors that in retrospect now appear as critical openings.

Hume, for example, may now be seen as having a rightful place — along with Nietzsche, Scheler, Peirce, Dewey, James, Whitehead, and, more recently, Robert Neville — in the critical protest against the Cartesian notion that reason can and should be a "pure" realm free from contamination by emotion, instinct, will, sentiment, and value. Within this protest, we see the development both of a "naturalist" *anthropology* of the Cartesian ideals of precision, certainty, and neutrality (Nietzche, Scheler, Dewey, and James), and a complementary *metaphysics* (Peirce, Whitehead, and Neville) in which "vagueness" as well as specificity, tentativeness, and valuation are honored as essential to thought.

In emphasizing the active, constructive nature of cognition, Kant undermined the Cartesian notion that the mind reflects and the scientist "reads off" what is simply *there* in the world. The Kantian "knower" is transcendental, of course, and Kant's "constructionism" begins and ends, like most Enlightenment thought, with a vision of universal law — in this case, the basic, ahistorical requirements of "knowability," represented by the categories. But the "Copernican Revolution in Thought," in asserting the activity of the subject, opened the door, paradoxically, to a more historical and contextual understanding of knowing. The knower, not the known, now comes under scrutiny — and not, as Descartes scrutinized the knower, for those contaminating elements which must be purged from cognition, but for those "active and interpreting forces," as Nietzsche says, "through which alone seeing becomes seeing *something*." The postulation of an inner "eye" in which these forces "are supposed to be lacking . . . [is] an absurdity and a nonsense" (1969, 119).

The articulation of the historical, social and cultural determinants of what Nietzsche called "perspective" can be seen as one paradigm of modern thought. The main theoretical categories of that paradigm have been worked out by various disciplines: the "philosophical anthropology" of Max Scheler, Karl Mannheim's work on ideology, and, historically fontal, the dialectical materialism of Karl Marx. Marx, of course, was not primarily interested in epistemological questions. But he is nonetheless the single most important philosophical figure in the development of modern historicism, with his emphasis on the historical nature of all human activity and thought and our frequent "false consciousness" of this. It was Marx who turned the tables on the Enlightenment, encouraging suspicion of all ideas that claim to represent universal, fundamental, "inherent," or "natural" features of reality.

The Cartesian ideal of the detached, purely neutral observer is here viewed as a type of mystification, and the ideals of absolute objectivity and ultimate foundations seen as requiring historical examination. In the modern era, "universal" after "universal" has fallen, under the scrutiny of Marxists, anthropologists, critical theorists, feminists, philosophers of science, and deconstructionists. The various claims regarding human nature and human sexuality (the "naturalness" of competition, the "necessity" of sexual repression, the "biological" nature of gender differences) have been challenged. Rorty and Foucault, respectively, have argued that the "mind" and "sexuality" are historical "inventions." And Patrick Heelan has shown that our most basic perceptions of space have a cultural history.

None of this signals the end of philosophy. What it *has* meant, however, is that it is extremely difficult today for the Cartesian philosopher to sit comfortably on the throne of the cultural overseer, "neutrally" legislating "how rational agreement can be reached" and where others have gone astray. The ideal of absolute intellectual purity and the belief in a clear and distinct universe are passing, though not without protest, out of the discipline. It is too soon to tell what sort of impact feminist and other reconstructions will have on the future development of philosophy, not to mention on the general intellectual and political life of our culture. But what does seem clear

Notes

INTRODUCTION

1. Descartes's original account of these dreams is lost, but a description of them may be found in Stern, *The Flight from Woman*, pp. 80–84. Although philosophers have generally accepted Descartes's interpretation of these dreams on face value, Stern and other psychoanalytically oriented thinkers have subjected them to a deeper scrutiny. (See Stern, pp. 84–89; Freud; Feuer; Scharfstein; and Wisdon.)

2. See Bordo, "The Cultural Overseer and the Tragic Hero" (pp. 181–183); Rorty (pp. 317–318); Cohen (p. 7).

3. Among the professional philosophers mentioned earlier, Avner Cohen and Bruce Wilshire have taken the psychological turn most seriously and literally. They are unusual within a discipline that has been as antipsychological as it has been antihistorical. It has generally been feminism — both French and American — that has been most penetrating and systematic in application of psychological and psychoanalytic categories to the history of thought. For both French and American feminists, the figure or the "pre-Oedipal" mother is central. French feminists have tended to emphasize the repression of the feminine in patriarchal culture and thought. A central target of criticism is "logocentric" discourse, contrasted to the more bodily, spontaneous discourse (the "semiotic" level) of early mother/infant relations. (See Elaine Marks and Isabelle Courtivron eds., *New French Feminisms*, and Shirley Garner, Claire Kahane and Madelon Sprengnether, eds., *The [M]other Tongue*.) American feminists have been drawn more to the British "object-relations" school, which emphasizes the development of self in relation to others. Often elaborating on the work of Nancy Chodorow, they have developed a fertile theoretical framework for exploring gender differences in early infant development, and their implications for male-dominated culture. The central target of criticism here has been the overvaluing of autonomy in our Western models of reason. (See especially Evelyn Fox Keller, but also articles by Naomi Scheman and Jane Flax in *Discovering Reality*, Sandra Harding and Merill B. Hintikka, eds.) The feminist who spans these divisions and whose work laid the ground for the development of many of these perspectives is, of course, Dorothy Dinnerstein, whose brilliant *The Mermaid and the Minotaur* was the first to connect psychoanalytic theory, gender, and culture.

ONE. THE PERVASIVENESS OF CARTESIAN ANXIETY

1. See Popkin (1979) for an excellent discussion of this revival. Popkin's book is an outstanding exception to the general tendency among contemporary philosophers to fail to take Cartesian skepticism seriously enough.

2. See Kenny, 1968, p. 24; Williams, p. 56; Harries, p. 31; and Gewirth, p. 389.

3. Margaret Wilson is a notable exception to this. Rightly emphasizing the radical nature of Descartes's mistrust of the senses, she recognizes that there is "experiential significance" in hyperbolic doubt, no matter how purposefully undertaken it is by Descartes (pp. 10, 34, and 228).

4. This sort of move occurs so frequently, in so many different contexts, that to lay it at the doorstep of particular authors would amount to philosophical scapegoating. I will, rather, refer to individual authors only in the context of discussion of their particular arguments.

5. Malcolm finds no problem with the notion that one may *dream* — e.g., that one is sitting by the fire. What he denies is that this is the same as *thinking*, in sleep, that one is sitting by the fire.

6. Working largely with a passage from the replies to Arnauld, in which Descartes distinguishes between "those matters that in actual truth we clearly perceive from those that we remember to have formerly perceived" (II, 115), Doney (1955) and others (e.g., Stout, 1967) have suggested that what is at issue for Descartes is the unreliability of memory (rather than the capacity to distinguish between the clear and distinct and the obscure and confused, "reason," or any other general cognitive capability). According to this argument, we can be certain, while "attending" to a proof, of its clearness and distinctness (and hence, its truth). But we cannot be sure that what we remember to have perceived clearly and distinctly was *in fact* so perceived. We need God, therefore, to certify, not the truth of present clear and distinct perceptions, but the reliability of our memory of proofs too cumbersome to be grasped "at once." No insidious mystification or general mental corruption here. What is at question is only the mind's ability to discriminate which remembered perceptions *were* clear and distinct.

    It is so difficult to reconcile this interpretation with so much in the text of the *Meditations* that one wonders what motivates Doney here. The footwork that is required to make sense, on this interpretation, of Descartes's doubt about simple mathematical and geometric operations is remarkable. Doney tries to account for these doubts by persuading us that Descartes believed those operations to require memory. Thus, he tries to discount Descartes's doubt about the reliability of his belief that a square has four sides (I, 147–8) by denying that it is a simple intuition. His argument rests on the claim that counting the sides of a square is an operation that "takes some time," that it is possible to forget how many sides you have counted in the middle of the operation, and so on (p. 329). But on the contrary, there is no evidence to support the idea that Descartes did not conceive of geometric operations of this sort as the simplest kinds of beliefs. (See HR, I, 7–8, 158, 147–8.)

7.   And having remarked that there was nothing at all in the statement 'I think, therefore I am' which assures me of having thereby made a true assertion, excepting that I see very clearly that to think it is necessary to be, I came to the conclusion that I might assume, as a general rule, that

the things which we conceive very clearly and distinctly are all true . . . (HR, I, 102).

8. See, for example, Williams, Hintikka, Flage, and Gombay.

TWO. THE EPISTEMOLOGICAL INSECURITY OF THE CARTESIAN ERA

1. Among those most often emphasized are the dominant notion of the universe as vast and complex but *limited* (Koyré), belief in the permanence of social and institutional arrangements (Huizinga), and the view that knowledge was already completed in its most essential aspects (Lewis, Koestler).

2. I am accepting Cornford's interpretation (pp. 48–51) that the theory of perception described is Plato's own. The *Theatetus*, by the way, provides a remarkable number of points for comparison and contrast with the *Meditations*, which I will not deal with but only mention here: Madmen, dreamers, an argument for the "infallibility" of sensation-in-itself, all have a place in the dialogue.

3. I am not in a position to speculate on all the cultural sources of this transformation. Obviously the invention of the telescope was of importance in indicting the naked senses as chief sources of human error (See Koyré, 90). Timothy Reiss suggests that the telescope gave rise to the metaphor of a distancing "space" between mind and material world "which was to haunt, directly or indirectly, much of the imaginative writing of the following century" (p. 4). The "space" symbolized by the telescope is thus the external counterpart of the distorting "inner space" of subjectivity. The only reliable mediator stands "outside" the subject; that which stands "within" is the source of confusion and error.

4. See Karsten Harries, "Descartes, Perspective and the Angelic Eye," for a discussion of this cultural deepening of interest in the phenomenon of perspective.

5. Carletti exclaims in amazement, of the Chinese: " . . . every invention for good or for evil, of beauty or ugliness, must have come from that region, or at least it can be affirmed that they have in themselves the knowledge of everything, not having had it from us or from the Greeks or other nations who taught it to us, but from native creators in that huge and very ancient country" (in Hale, 1967, pp. 342–43).

6. McLuhan, as one might expect, views printing as essential to this transformation. Print, he says, "enabled a people to see [its] vernacular for the first time" (p. 138) and thus to see itself for the first time. Through print, the culture is thus able to discover that it has a "point of view" (p. 221).

THREE. THE EMERGENCE OF INWARDNESS

1. For Piaget, "egocentrism" has a very different meaning from our ordinary use of the term. Far from signifying an absorption with the self, for Piaget "egocentrism" characterizes that stage prior to the development of a sense of self. The

sense of *world* has also not yet developed — hence, the somewhat misleading term, "*egocentrism.*"

2. Piaget proposes this correspondence in a number of places, but it is worked out most systematically in *Insights and Illusions of Philosophy* (1965), *Structuralism* (1968b), and *Genetic Epistemology* (1970).

3. In Greek, as Rorty points out, there is no way to divide "conscious states" from events in an external world (p. 47).

4. See Cohen, "Descartes, Consciousness and Depersonalization: Viewing the History of Philosophy from a Strausian Perspective", for an extremely interesting and insightful discussion of this alienation of self and world. For a vivid contemporary example of how deeply the Cartesian schism between "inner" and "external" reality still grips philosophy, even as it attempts to abandon Cartesian absolutism, see Thomas Nagel, *The View From Nowhere.*

FOUR. LOCATEDNESS AND INDIVIDUATION

1. Although the science of optics itself is as old as Euclid, and there had been intense Western interest in optics from the time of the recovery of Euclid's *Optica* in the thirteenth century, there is no evidence of any other culture before the European Renaissance applying it to pictorial representation. (Ivins, 318; McLuhan, 56; Baxandall, 143) *Foreshortening* had been done before — by the Greeks, and quite commonly in the late Gothic art — but it was learned and taught from a pattern model, not from a method of perspective construction. That these cultures had developed techniques of rendering *depth* is indisputable; but the systematic construction of three-dimensional space, as seen from a fixed point of view, on a two-dimensional canvas is quite another thing. Even in the most "realistic" Greek paintings, as Panofsky says, "space and things do not coalesce into a unified whole nor does the space seem to extend beyond our range of vision" (p. 122).

2. There was also a hierarchy of colors (for example, specifying which blue to use for Mary's robe was often part of the specific instructions given by patrons to painters) and a code of gestures. An extraordinary degree of "participation" — in interpreting this symbolism — was thus required of the viewer of a medieval painting. Of course, these "meanings" were conventionally known, and such interpretation was virtually automatic (Baxandall, 82).

3. Gibson points out that it is very difficult for us to see the coverging lines represented by the right and left margins of a paper lying in front of us even *when* we fixate on the scene.

4. Medievals, after all, were not used to viewing pictorial representations, in the way that we are: framed (sometimes, distractingly framed) and set off against a background — e.g., a living room or museum wall — whose ambience is often jarringly discontinuous with the ambience of the picture. They were used to

viewing representations that were not only often *physically* continuous with the environment (e.g. church frescoes) but whose "message" was in harmony with the surroundings and designed to be part of a unified spiritual experience. The secularization of painting, on the other hand, brought artworks into environments in which they stood out as visual "islands" in the midst of an ongoing domestic life directed toward things other than contemplation.

5. It is speculation about the geocentricity of our perspective, for example, as Harries points out, that lead Cusanus to question the notion that there is any natural center to the universe and hence any limits (pp. 30–31). And Mario Moussa suggests that perspective "geometrized space," and so led to the postulation of infinity: "[I]nfinity is simply the next step after geometrization; there is no reason for a straight line to stop at any given point and so it does not stop at all. Straight lines shattered the spheres of the medieval universe" (p. 21).

6. "Perspecktive als 'symbolische Form'". This essay remains untranslated into English at this date. My brief discussion of it is indebted, therefore, to the discussions by Edgerton (pp. 153–59) and Heelan.

7. See essay six of this study for further discussion of the "receptacle" of the *Timeaus*.

8. This use of "perspective" as a cognitive metaphor is particularly interesting when we notice that from its origins in the science of optics — to which the term "perspective" originally referred — through its development as a convention of pictorial representation, the most prominent connotations of "perspectivity" had been positive. *Perspicere* itself means "to see clearly," and the geometrical laws of optics were regarded, in the Middle Ages, as a reflection of God's manner of spreading His Grace throughout the universe. Alberti, who was the first to formally record the principles of the application of optics to artistic representation (1435), applauded this new conception of pictorial space "within which," as Edgerton describes it, "painted figures could be represented gracefully, according to the harmonious rhythms of geometry," in a "world of order" (p. 30). Dante describes perspective as the "handmaid" of geometry: "lily-white, unspotted by error and most certain" (Baxandall, 124). And Peter Limoges, in *On the Moral and Spiritual Eye*, compares the "direct lines of sight" of the perspective painting to the clear moral vision of the Godly person (Baxandall, 105).

The "point of view" of the perspective painting is, of course, a "fiction," providing an ideal vantage which anyone can adopt. In life, as the seventeenth century appeared to be discovering, the "point of view" is inescapable, personal, shifting, and affords no such vantage. The earliest speculation on the perspectivity of human experience, according to Harries, can be found in Cusanus's questioning of the geocentric cosmology; is not such a cosmology, Cusanus suggests, the result of the inevitable "geocentricity" of our point of view as inhabitants of the earth (Harries, 30–31). But Cusanus here, as often, was exceptional in his own time. It is only in the sixteenth and seventeenth centuries that the implications of "perspectivity" as a fact of human experience begin to fully emerge and that the notion of "perspective" as a cognitive metaphor for epistemological limitation and isolation becomes popular (Guillen, 315–317).

9. *The Garden of Prayer* (1454) instructs young girls to imagine places well-known to them and to "map" the story of the Passion, using the images of people they know to represent Jesus, St. Peter, St. John, Mary Magdalene, and so on (Baxandall, 46).

10. He goes on: "The directions 'up' and 'down' are no longer absolute, nor are weight and bouyancy. The 'weight' of a stone meant, before, its tendency to fall toward the center of the earth; that was the meaning of 'gravity.' Now the sun and moon become centers of gravity of their own. There are no longer any absolute directions in space. The universe had lost its core. It no longer has a heart, but a thousand hearts."

FIVE. PURIFICATION AND TRANSCENDENCE IN THE MEDITATIONS

1. Even to assert the fact of infinity, for Descartes, is to transcend the bounds of human knowledge. For, although it "is impossible to prove or even to conceive that there are bounds to the matter of which the world is made," there may nonetheless be limits "which are known to God though inconceivable to me" (PL, 221). The most we can say about the extent of the universe is that it is "from [our] own point of view . . . indefinite"; only God can be "positively conceive[d] as infinite" (PL, 242), since this infinity is necessarily contained in his essence. And even the "positive" knowledge that God is infinite does not entail the ability to "grasp" the infinite. For, although we are certain that God, unlike the universe, can have no limits (*Principle* XXVII, HR, I, 230):

    > . . . our soul, being finite, cannot comprehend or conceive Him. In the same way we can touch a mountain with our hands but we cannot put our arms around it as we could put them around a tree or something else not too large for them. To comprehend something is to embrace it in one's thought; to know something it is sufficient to touch it with one's thought (To Mersenne, May 27, 1630, PL, 15. See also Reply, I, II, 18).

    By virtue of our finitude, then — although we can "touch" the infinite with our thought — we can neither completely comprehend the scope of the universe nor can we comprehend the infinite *qua* infinite. Neither of these limitations disturbs Descartes; indeed, they are essential to his system: If the human being's comprehension were *not* limited, neither of the third Meditation's proofs of the existence of God could gain a foothold. For, the proof from the idea of God depends upon my recognition that I lack the formal reality (infinite goodness, wisdom, and power) required for *me* to be the cause of the idea of a being with such qualities. And the "causal" argument depends upon the same recognition, but as entailing the necessity of postulating something other than *me* as the cause of myself (for if it had been me, why would I have created myself so imperfect?) (HR, I, 168).

2. Mary Douglas (1966, 1982) has written of the frequency with which social orders are demarcated into a pure "us" and a taboo "them" group. The strategy not

only allows the projection of responsibility for disorder onto the outsider group, it also, as Richard Sennet has emphasized, confers the illusion of stable identity and solidarity on the insider group — "the pleasure in recognizing 'us' and 'who we are'" (p. 31). Bruce Wilshire, in a profound and insightful study of the development of professionalism in academia, has explored how these dynamics function, albeit in disguised and mystified form, in the extreme insularity of professional academic disciplines (*Professionalism and the Eclipse of University Teaching: Dynamics of Purification and Exclusion*, manuscript in progress).

3. *The Cartesian Doctrine of Freedom.* See Kenny, 1972, p. 8.

4. To exonerate God from responsibility for error, as Kenny points out, it would have been sufficient for Descartes to have made judgment a *voluntary* act of the intellect (as walking is a voluntary act of the body). He needn't have gone so far as to make it an act of the *will*. Imagining and conceiving, for example, appear to be such voluntary acts of the intellect for Descartes. They require the participation of the will (see *Passions of the Soul*, HR, I, 340; PL, 177–78), but are not themselves *acts* of the will. Judgment is, and Kenny puzzles over this, suggesting that it may have something to do with Descartes's desire to preserve a continuity between error and moral fault (1972, p. 8). Without disagreeing with this, I want to note that if the exoneration of the *intellect* is an aim of the fourth Meditation, this could *not* be accomplished by making judgment a voluntary act of the intellect. It requires a "relocation" of the sources of error to an arena distinct from the intellect.

5. "Dirt-affirming" philosophies, by contrast, are those within whose system everything actual has a function. For James, Hegel is the paradigm example of this. (Douglas, 1982, p. 164)

6. There has been a scholarly debate about whether this capacity of clear and distinct ideas to "determine" the will is in tension with the Cartesian doctrine of the will as infinite. Kenny (1972, p. 8) and Williams (p. 180) see this as a genuine tension. Hiram Caton, on the other hand, resolves the apparent contradiction by noting that for Descartes, truth and falsity are not "symmetrical values in a binary matrix" (p. 92). Rather, he maintains, Descartes holds to a *rationalist* theory of truth, in which "judgement plays no role" and "clear ideas are known to be true *per se*," and a *voluntarist* theory of error, in which judgment is required for the commission of error (p. 93). Although I do not wish to comment on this debate as such, my own reading of the fourth Meditation, as presented in this essay, can be seen to have a greater affinity with Caton's views on the matter.

7. These function in the context of epistemological "purification rituals" for authors other than Descartes, too. Evelyn Fox Keller, in her inspired and fascinating reading of Bacon's *Masculine Birth of Time*, attempts to correct the popular misconception that seventeenth-century science is *only* about aggression and control of nature, by focusing on Bacon's model of mind, which, like Descartes's, emphasizes the ideals of *submissiveness* and *receptivity* to the "true

native rays" of things. To achieve this receptivity, however, requires that the mind first purify and cleanse *itself* of "idols" and "false preconceptions." As Keller describes Bacon's project:

> To receive God's truth, the mind must be pure and clean, submissive and open. Only then can it give birth to a masculine and virile science. That is, if the mind is pure, receptive, and submissive in its relation with God, it can be transformed by God into a forceful, potent, and virile agent in its relation to nature. Cleansed of contamination, the mind can be impregnated by God and, in that act, virilized: made potent and capable of generating virile offspring in its union with Nature (p. 38).

8. Although Descartes maintains that the emotions can "indirectly" be governed by the will (e.g., through the decision to try to "reason through" or talk oneself out of a particular fear [I, 352]), we can never simply will ourselves *not* to be afraid, or depressed, or jealous. Once an emotion is experienced, "the most that the will can do . . . is not to yield to its effects and to restrain many of the movements to which it disposes the body" (I, 252).

9. Phenomenologically, the distinguishing feature of acts of the pure intellect is, besides their lack of imagic content (PL, 107), that they formed through *reflection of the mind on itself* (see to Mersenne, October 16, 1639, PL, 66). This is not to say that they are formed through reflection on *thinking*. Rather, the exercise of pure intellect is an inquiry into the *ideas* of the mind (e.g., of the idea of the wax, of the self, of God, of mind, of body). It is an investigation which sets as its goal what the mind *cannot conceive* the object in question as being without, lest the object cease to be what it is (Gewirth, 1955, pp. 271-273). This, determined through a rigorous series of "reductions," as Gewirth calls them, in which the mind has "reduced [ideas] to their elements and tried to separate and combine them in various ways" will be the essence of the object, its "true and immutable nature" (in Doney, 276).(Thus, God cannot be conceived without existence, nor wax without extension, nor myself without thought, etc.)

   This operation, if performed successfully, will result in the conviction that the mind has reached the limits of its freedom of imagination and will: It will find itself coerced and compelled "by the internal meaning of ideas" (Gewirth, 1955, p. 274). But it is important to note that the culminating compulsion is reached as a result of an arduous and deliberately undertaken process; the mind must *subject* itself to the coerciveness exercised by the internal meanings of ideas. To do this it has to learn to "see" with *its* eye and not that of the body.

10. See footnote #1 for a discussion of the Cartesian limits to human understanding.

11. The male pronoun is the appropriate one here, as we shall see in the next essay.

SIX. THE CARTESIAN MASCULINIZATION OF THOUGHT

1. Bossuet, too, believed that the sense-rule of childhood represents something

"depraved in the common source of our birth" (Harth, 218). LaRochefoucault called childhood "a perpetual intoxication, a fever on the brain" (Harth, 219). In a popular treatise on education, written in 1646, Balthazar Gratién writes of "that insipidity of childhood which disgusts the sane mind; that coarseness of youth which finds pleasure in scarcely anything but material objects and which is only a very crude sketch of the man of thought . . . Only time can cure a person of childhood and youth, which are truly ages of imperfection in every respect" (Ariès, 131–32).

2. Since the body is the *res extensa* of the human being, as mechanical in its operations as a machine (see II, 104; I, 116), this means that our purely bodily existence is not only less than "truly human," but is comparable to animal existence. Animals, as Descartes is notorious for maintaining, are mere automata (PL, 53–54, 121, 206–8, 243–45; HR, I, 117), and had we not the evidence of the human being's extraordinary flexibility of response (as demonstrated by the adaptability of language and reason to particular circumstances) we would have no reason to think otherwise of human beings either (HR, I, 116).

3. See Dinnerstein, Hillman, Brown, Marcuse, Stern, and Griffin, among many others.

4. As this book goes to press, Harding's eagerly-awaited *The Science Question in Feminism* (Cornell University Press) is just being released, too late for inclusion as one of the works surveyed in this essay. Harding's contribution to contemporary discussions of modern science, especially among philosophers, is very important.

5. See Keller, Merchant, and Easlea for excellent discussions of the Baconian imagery of nature.

6. These themes are symbolically represented, as I have argued elsewhere, in the structures of tragedy and comedy. There, we find all the elements of the "infant" drama: the pain of individuation, the dream of lost union, and (as in Descartes) the attempt to triumph over one's (unchosen) birth through the denial of its power over the "self-made" self. The meaning of the mother, and of the "feminine," in all this was not discovered by Freud either, as he recognized. Throughout tragedy and comedy, the woman (and most particularly, the mother) represents the historical roots of the self, the authority of the flesh, and the dangers (for tragedy) and joys (for comedy) of union with another. The desire for mastery through individuation, on the other hand, is "masculine" — and we may now recognize it as strikingly Cartesian, too: the project of the self-making self in willful repudiation of historical and familial ties, the limitations of the body, and the power of the flesh. In *Oedipus*, all these come together, which Freud, of course, saw. He emphasized, however, rather the wrong point. The spiritual center of the classic Oedipal story is not the desire to sleep with one's mother, but to become the father of oneself, to be the creator rather than the helpless pawn in the drama of one's own life. (See Bordo, "The Cultural Overseer and the Tragic Hero", *Soundings*, 1982).

7. This is the social reality behind the witch-hunters' fantasies of female power. The fact is that a great many of the women accused of witchcraft *were* involved in conception and birth, as well as all other aspects of sickness and health. They, indeed, *did* have control (though not of the sort fantasized by Kramer and Sprenger), for healing had traditionally been the province of women, and, in the case of midwifery, remained overwhelmingly so until the eighteenth century (Rich, 121). These female lay-healers, according to Ehrenreich and English, were "singled out particularly" in the witch hunts (p. 36). Called "good witches," they were condemned even more strongly than the "bad." But "the greatest injuries to the Faith as regards the heresy of witches are done by mid-wives" (Kramer and Sprenger). Why? First, because they relieved women of the curse of Eve's original sin, through the use of ergot to dull the pain of childbirth (in 1591, Agnes Simpson was burned for just this crime) (Rich, 117). Second, because they were able to control miscarriage through the use of Belladonna (Ehrenreich and English, 37). It was not until the seventeenth century, however, that midwifery finally begins to give way to the male practice of "obstetrics," described by Suzanne Arms as the final stage in "the gradual attempt by man to extricate the processes of birth from women and call it his own" (Rich, 90).

8. It was male practitioners who established the lying-down position for women in labor, rendering women passive and dependent in the process of birth (Rich, 137), and who, in the late sixteenth century, invented and promulgated the use of forceps in delivery. For Adrienne Rich, the "hands of iron" which replace the "hands of flesh" of the female midwives "symbolize the art of the obstetrician" (p. 133). They began to be used promiscuously, preparation for control over possible difficulty becoming the too-routine practice of such control (as has happened similarly today with the Caesarean section). Midwives campaigned against the overuse and abuse of the forceps (Rich, 137–41). They themselves, of course, could not use the forceps, which was a technology available only to the licensed physician, and there is no doubt an element of political battle at work here. But even the strongest feminists among the midwives argued for the intervention of the male physician when complications arose; it was chiefly against the premature use of forceps, to shorten delivery time, and against their clumsy use, by male surgeons inexperienced at deliveries, that the midwives railed. Male physicians, most notable among them being William Harvey, mounted, in return, a ferocious campaign against midwives (Merchant, 153–55).

9. The fact that there were more female than male witches was linked to the excessive carnality of the female. "All witchcraft comes from carnal lust, which is in women insatiable," say Kramer and Sprenger (Easlea, 80). This view of women was not idiosyncratic, as Easlea points out, citing Walter Charleton's *Ephesian Matron* (1659) and Burton's *Anatomy of Melancholy* (1621). "You are the true Hiena's," says Charleton, "that allure us with the fairness of your

> skins; and when folly hath brought us within your reach, you leap upon us and devour us. You are the traitors to Wisdom; the impediment to Industry . . . the clogs to virtue, and goads to drive us all to Vice, Impiety, and Ruine. You are the Fools Paradise, the Wisemans Plague, and the grand Error of Nature" (Easlea, 242).

"Of women's unnatural, insatiable lust, what country, what village doth not complain" notes Burton (Easlea, 242). It is for the sake of fulfilling the insatiable "mouth of the womb," according to Sprenger and Kramer, that "they consort even with the devil" (Easlea, 8). The accusation of copulation with the devil was a common charge at witch trials, and the rampant eroticism of the witch a common theme of paintings on the subject (Merchant, 134).

10. This is the widely accepted "animalculist" version. In the much less influential "ovist" version, the animacules are placed in the woman's womb by God at the time of creation. In either version, the original source of the animacules is God. The virtue of preformation and embôitement, for the mechanists, was its thoroughly mechanical solution to the vexing problem of generation: If the body is pure *res extensa*, and if *res extensa* is barren and nonsentient, how does a sentient human being develop out of it? The new reproductive theory enabled the imaging of the sentient human being as being merely "housed" within matter, and not as developing out of it, its true father acknowledged as God.

11. Dorothy Dinnerstein discusses, at some length, what she takes to be the psychological sources of the dominant cultural equation of femaleness and the natural world. We first encounter the mother "before we are able to distinguish between a center of sentience and an impersonal force of nature" (p. 106). As we grow to learn the distinction, she claims, our associations to each remain contaminated by this ancient "confusion." The woman remains something less-than-human (in contrast to the father, whom we come to know from the start as a distinct center of independent subjectivity) and nature remains something more than an "impersonal" force. "She" is also a female force, of course, since it was from the mother that she was originally indistinguishable.

But women not only remain *associated* with nature. They also, claims Dinnerstein, become a natural target for all later rage *against* nature. "Like nature, which sends blizzards and locusts as well as sunshine and strawberries," the mother (and later, women in general) is perceived "as capricious, sometimes actively malevolent. Her body is the first important piece of the physical world that we encounter, and the events for which she seems responsible the first instances of fate. Hence mother nature, with her hurricane daughters . . . hence that fickle female, Lady Luck" (p. 95).

12. That which appears as mysterious and powerful may not always be regarded as dreadful or as requiring *taming*. The unpredictable caprice of fortune, for example, was believed to rule earthly life in the Middle Ages — but its vicissitudes were regarded in a spirit of acceptance (Lewis, 139–40). For Machiavelli, in contrast, "Fortune is a woman, and it is necessary if you wish to master her, to conquer her by force" (Merchant, 130). And, while the evidence for there having been true matriarchal cultures is debated, the existence of what Rich calls *gynocentric* cultures — cultures in which women were venerated, not feared, for their strength and power, especially in their maternal function — is unquestionable (Rich, 80–89; Sanday, 15–33, 113–128). Moreover, that which appears as mysterious and powerful may not always be experienced as decisively "not-

self." The Middle Ages, while hardly a gynocentric culture, *was* a culture in which the mystery and power of nature did not appear as the whim of an alien "other."

13. Knowledge "by sympathy," as Karl Stern says, has its "natural fundament" in the "primary bond with the mother" (p. 54). But mothers, according to Chodorow, treat their female children and male children differently. Identification and symbiosis with daughters tends to be stronger. Daughters, in response, tend to perceive *themselves* as more closely identified with the mother, less distinct from her, and more comfortable, in adult life, with experiences of "merger" with others. By contrast, boys are experienced by their mothers as a "male opposite," and are more likely to have had to "curtail their primary love and sense of empathic tie with their mother" (pp. 166–67). Moreover, for the boy, issues of diffrentiation from the mother become intertwined with issues of gender identification. "Dependence on his mother, attachment to her, and identification with her represent that which is not masculine; a boy must reject dependence and deny attachment and identification" (p. 181). The result, according to Chodorow, is that "girls emerge . . . with a basis for 'empathy' built into their primary definition of self in a way that boys do not" (p. 167). The analysis is not only developmental, but institutional, for the proposed differences in male and female modes of knowing all hinge on the institution of female nurturing.

14. An examination of the relevance of this contemporary developmental explanation to the Cartesian era must fall to the sociologist and historian of the family. No doubt Ariès's profound thesis that childhood itself was not "discovered" until the sixteenth century has some relevance here, for until that time, as Ariès argues, very little in the way of nurturing of *either* sex went on. It is in the sixteenth and seventeenth centuries, therefore, that we might expect the developmental processes described by Chodorow to begin to have some striking application. My own study here is certainly suggestive of the fruitfulness of further investigation along these lines.

15. See, especially, the final chapter in Gilligan, in which it becomes clear that Gilligan is calling, not for a "feminization" of knowledge, from which more masculinist modes are excluded, but the recognition that each, cut off from the other, founders on its own particular reefs, just as it offers its own partial truths about human experience.

16. See, as a striking example, Ian Hacking's review of Keller's *Gender and Science*. Hacking is obviously unaware of the long feminist literature (including Keller's own earlier work) in which Keller's volume of essays is grounded, and apparently considers the notion that gender has influenced the construction of fact and theory to be an idea that has burst forth, for the first time, with the publication of this 1985 collection. He also is unwilling to accept Keller's own identification of herself as a radical feminist (apparently, for Hacking, the term cannot refer to anyone whose work he appreciates, and must always signal crude and negative thinking). He is genuinely taken, however, with the revolutionary import and the potential cultural value of work such as Keller's.

17. See Harding and Hintikka, *Discovering Reality*, and Alison Jaggar, *Feminist Politics and Human Nature*, chapter 11. French feminism has its own traditions of conceptual reconstruction; see Marks and Courtivron, *New French Feminisms*. Recently, conferences and seminars, explicitly organized around themes of "revisioning" or reconstructing ethics and epistemology, have begun to appear. To cite just two examples: Seminars entitled "Feminist Reconstructions of Self and Society" and "Feminist Ways of Knowing" were held in 1985 at Douglass College, Rutgers University; a conference entitled "Women and Moral Theory" was held in March, 1985 at the State University of New York at Stony Brook. Papers delivered at the Douglass seminar included topics such as the role of emotions in knowing, non-dualist perspectives on knowledge, the role of the body, and the role of "care" in morality. A collection of these papers — *Feminist Reconstructions of Being and Knowing* — is now in preparation (editors Alison Jaggar and Susan Bordo, Rutgers University Press). The Stony Brook conference was devoted to an exploration of the work of Carol Gilligan and its intellectual implications. Several papers presented offered Gilligan-inspired reconstructions of ethical theory.

18. It seems clear that so long as masculine values continue to exert their grip on the public domain, there are severe constraints on the potential that women may bring, as they enter that domain, to transform it. Many radical feminists fault liberal feminism, which has prioritized equal opportunity without a corresponding emphasis on the need for cultural transformation, with contributing to more of a "masculinization" than "feminization" of contemporary culture. Women have been "allowed" in the public domain, but they have been required to adopt the values of that domain. On the other hand, unless the promotion of "feminine" values is consistently and explicitly wedded to a critique of the sexual division of labor, it may operate as a justification and romanticization of that division of labor, and a banner under which women can be encouraged to return to (or remain in) the private sphere where "their" virtues flourish. The critique of cultural values must always be joined to a recognition of the "material" inequalities and power imbalances that those values serve. But the cultural critique is essential. Without it, women surrender the power of our "critical alterity" (as Ynestra King calls it) to be instrumental in the realization of a different social and intellectual order.

Bibliography

Alberti, Leon Battista. *On Painting*. New Haven: Yale University Press, 1956.

Alexander, Robert. "The Problem of Metaphysical Doubt and its Removal." In *Cartesian Studies*, pp. 106–22. Edited by R. J. Butler. New York: Barnes & Noble, 1972.

Ariès, Philippe. *Centuries of Childhood: A Social History of Family Life*. New York: Vintage, 1962.

Aristotle. *Basic Works*. Edited by Richard McKeon. New York: Random House, 1941.

Ashworth, E. J. "Descartes' Theory of Clear and Distinct Ideas." In *Cartesian Studies*, pp. 89–105. Edited by R. J. Butler. New York: Barnes & Noble, 1972.

Augustine. *Works*. Edited by Marcus Dods. Edinburgh: T. T. Clark Co., 1871–76.

Barfield, Owen. *Saving the Appearances: A Study in Idolatry*. New York: Harcourt Brace Jovanovich, n.d.

Baxandall, Michael. *Painting and Experience in Fifteenth Century Italy*. Oxford: Oxford University Press, 1972.

Beilin, Harry. "The Development of Physical Concepts." In *Cognitive Development and Epistemology*. Edited by Theodore Mischel. New York: Academic Press, 1971.

Bell, Susan Groag, ed. *Women: From the Greek to the French Revolution*. Stanford: Stanford University Press, 1973.

Berman, Morris. *The Re-enchantment of the World*. Ithaca; Cornell University Press, 1981.

Bernstein, Richard. "Philosophy in the Conversation of Mankind." *The Review of Metaphysics* 33, no. 4 (1980): 745–75.

Bordo, Susan. "The Cultural Overseer and the Tragic Hero: Comedic and Feminist Perspectives on the Hubris of Philosophy." *Soundings*, Vol. LXV, No. 2, Summer 1982, pp. 181–205.

Brown, Norman O. *Life Against Death*. New York: Random House, 1959.

Burtt, E. A. *The Metaphysical Foundations of Modern Science*. Garden City: Doubleday, 1941.

Butler, R. J., ed. *Cartesian Studies*. New York: Barnes & Noble, 1972.

Capra, Fritjof. *The Turning Point*. New York: Simon and Schuster, 1983.

Caton, Hiram. "Will and Reason in Descartes' Theory of Error." *Journal of Philosophy* 72, no. 4 (1975): 87–104.

Chamberlain, E. R. *Everyday Life in Renaissance Times*. New York: Capricorn, 1965.

Chodorow, Nancy. *The Reproduction of Mothering*. Berkeley: University of California Press, 1978.

———. "Family Structure and Feminine Personality." In *Woman, Culture and Society*, pp. 43–66. Edited by Michele Rosaldo and Louise Lamphere. Stanford: Stanford University Press, 1974.

Cohen, Avner. "Descartes, Consciousness and Depersonalization: Viewing the History of Philosophy from a Strausian Perspective." *The Journal of Medicine and Philosophy* 9 (1984), pp. 7–27.

Danto, Arthur. *What Philosophy Is*. New York: Harper and Row, 1968.

deBeauvoir, Simone. *The Second Sex*. New York: Alfred A. Knopf, 1957.

Descartes. *Philosophical Works*. Vols. I and II. Edited by Elizabeth Haldane and G. R. T. Ross. Cambridge: Cambridge University Press, 1969.

Descartes. *Conversations with Burman*. Translated by John Cottingham. Oxford: Clarendon Press, 1976.

Dewey, John. *Reconstruction in Philosophy*. 1920; reprint ed., Boston: Beacon Press, 1957.

———. *The Quest for Certainty*. 1929; reprint ed., New York: Capricorn, 1960.

Dinnerstein, Dorothy. *The Mermaid and the Minotaur*. New York: Harper and Row, 1977.

Doney, Willis. "The Cartesian Circle." *Journal of the History of Ideas* 16 (1955): 324–38.

———. ed. *Descartes: A Collection of Critical Essays*. Garden City: Doubleday, 1967.

Douglas, Mary. *Purity and Danger*. London: Routledge and Kegan Paul, 1966.

———. *Natural Symbols*. New York: Pantheon, 1982.

Easlea, Brian. *Witch-hunting, Magic and the New Philosophy*. Atlantic Highlands, N.J.: Humanities Press, 1980.

Edgerton, Jr., Samuel. *The Renaissance Rediscovery of Linear Perspective*. New York: Harper and Row, 1975.

Ehrenreich, Barbara, and Dierdre English. *For Her Own Good*. New York: Anchor/Doubleday, 1979.

Evan, J. L. "Error and the Will." *Philosophy* 38, no. 144 (1963): 136–48.

Farrington, Benjamin. *Temporis Partus Masculus: An Untranslated Writing of Francis Bacon*. Centaurus I, 1951.

Febvre, Lucièn. *Life in Renaissance France*. Cambridge: Harvard University Press, 1977.

Feuer, L. "The Dream of Descartes." *The American Imago*, 20, pp. 3–26.

Feyerabend, Paul. "Philosophy Today." In *Teaching Philosophy Today*. Edited by T. W. Bynum and S. Rosenberg. Bowling Green: Philosophical Documentation Center, n.d.

Flage, Daniel. "Descartes' Cogito". *History of Philosophy Quarterly*. Vol. 2, No. 2, April 1985, pp. 163–178.

Frankfurt, Harry. *Demons, Dreamers and Madmen*. New York: Bobbs-Merrill, 1970.

_____. "Descartes on the Consistency of Reason." In *Descartes: Critical and Interpretive Essays*, pp. 26–39. Edited by Michael Hooker. Baltimore: Johns Hopkins Press, 1978.

_____. "Descartes' Validation of Reason." In *Descartes: A Collection of Critical Essays*, pp. 209–226. Edited by Willis Doney. Garden City: Doubleday, 1967.

Freud, Sigmund. *Beyond the Pleasure Principle*. New York: Bantam, 1959.

Furth, Hans. *Piaget and Knowledge*. New Jersey: Prentice-Hall, 1969.

Galileo. *Discoveries and Opinions*. Edited by Stillman Drake. Garden City: Anchor, 1957.

Garner, Shirley Nelson; Kahane, Claine and Sprengnether, Madelon, *The (M)other Tongue*. Ithaca: Cornell University Press, 1985.

Gay, Peter. *The Bourgeois Experience*, vol. one, *Education of the Senses*. New York: Oxford University Press, 1984.

Gewirth, Alan. "The Cartesian Circle." *Philosophical Review* 50, no. 4 (1941): 368–95.

_____. "Clearness and Distinctness in Descartes." Doney, 1955, pp. 250–277.

Gibson, James J. *The Perception of the Visual World*. Boston: Houghton Mifflin, 1950.

Gilligan, Carol. *In a Different Voice*. Cambridge: Harvard University Press, 1982.

Gillispie, Charles. *The Edge of Objectivity*. Princeton: Princeton University Press, 1960.

Gilmore, Myron. "The Renaissance Conception of the Lessons of History." In *Facets of the Renaissance*, pp. 73–102. Edited by William Werkmeister. New York: Harper and Row, 1959.

Gombay, Andre. "Cogito Ergo Sum: Inference or Argument?" in Butler, 1972, pp. 71–88.

Gombrich, E. H. *Art and Illusion*. Princeton: Princeton University Press, 1961.

Greer, Germaine. *The Female Eunuch*. New York: McGraw-Hill, 1970.

Grene, Marjorie. *A Portrait of Aristotle*. Chicago: Chicago University Press, 1963.

Griffin, Susan. *Women and Nature*. New York: Harper and Row, 1978.

Guillen, Claudio. "On the Concept and Metaphor of Perspective." In *Literature As System*. Princeton: Princeton University Press, 1971.

Hacking, Ian. "Liberating the Laboratory." *The New Republic*, July 15 and 22, 1985, pp. 47–50.

Hale, J. R. *Renaissance Exploration*. New York: Norton, 1968.

———. "Geographical Horizons and Mental Horizons." In *The Age of the Renaissance*, pp. 317–43. Edited by Denis Hay. New York: McGraw Hill, 1967.

Hamlyn, D. W. "Epistemology and Conceptual Development." In *Cognitive Development and Epistemology*. New York: Academic Press, 1971.

Harding, Sandra. "Is Gender a Variable in Conceptions of Rationality?" *Dialectica*, 36, pp. 225–42.

——— and Hintikka, Merril. *Discovering Reality: Feminist Perspectives on Epistemology, Science, and Philosophy of Science*. Dordrecht: Reidel, 1983.

Harries, Karsten. "Descartes, Perspective and the Angelic Eye." *Yale French Studies*. no. 49 (1973): 28–42.

Harth, Erica. "Classical Innateness." *Yale French Studies*, no. 49 (1973): 212–30.

Hay, Denis, ed. *The Age of the Renaissance*. New York: McGraw-Hill, 1967.

Heelan, Patrick. *Space-Perception and the Philosophy of Science*. Berkeley: University of California Press, 1983.

Heidegger, Martin. *An Introduction to Metaphysics*. Translated by Ralph Manheim. Garden City: Doubleday, 1961.

Hillman, James. *The Myth of Analysis*. New York: Harper and Row, 1972.

Hintikka, Jaako. "Cogito Ergo Sum: Inference or Performance?" In Doney, 1967, pp. 108–139.

Hooker, Michael, ed. *Descartes: Critical and Interpretive Studies*. Baltimore: Johns Hopkins Press, 1978.

Huizinga, J. *The Waning of the Middle Ages*. Garden City: Anchor, 1949.

Ivins, William M. *Art and Geometry*. New York: Dover, 1946.

———. *On the Rationalization of Sight*. New York: DaCapo Press, 1973.

Jaggar, Alison. *Feminist Politics and Human Nature*. New Jersey: Rowman and Allanheld, 1983.

James, William. *The Varieties of Religious Experience*. 1901; printed ed. London, 1952.

———. *The Will to Believe and Other Essays*. 1897; printed ed., New York: Dover, 1956.

Keller, Evelyn Fox. *Reflections on Gender and Science*. New Haven: Yale University Press, 1985.

Kenny, Anthony. *Descartes: A Study of His Philosophy*. New York: Random House, 1968.

_____. "Descartes on Ideas." In *Descartes: A Collection of Critical Essays*, pp. 227–49. Edited by Willis Doney. Garden City: Doubleday, 1967.

_____. ed. *Descartes: Philosophical Letters*. Minneapolis: University of Minnesota Press, 1970.

_____. "Descartes on the Will." In *Cartesian Studies*, pp. 1–31. Edited by R. J. Butler. New York: Barnes & Noble, 1972.

Kepes, Gyorgy. *Language of Vision*. Chicago: Paul Theobald, 1949.

Klein, Melanie. "Early Stages of the Oedipus Conflict." In *The World of the Child*. ed. by Toby Talbot, New York: Jason Aronson, 1974, pp. 98–111.

Koestler, Arthur. *The Sleepwalkers*. New York: Grosset & Dunlap, 1959.

Koyré, Alexander. *From the Closed World to the Infinite Universe*. Baltimore: Johns Hopkins Press, 1957.

Krell, David. "Memory and Malady in Freud and Hegel." Philosophy Colloquia Series, State University of New York at Stony Brook, February 23, 1979.

Kroner, Richard. *Speculation and Revelation in Modern Philosophy*. Philadelphia: Westminster, 1961.

Lamprecht, Sterling. *Our Philosophical Traditions*. New York: Appleton Century, 1955.

Lederer, Wolfgang. *The Fear of Women*. New York: Harcourt Brace, 1968.

Lewis, C. S. *The Discarded Image*. Cambridge: Cambridge University Press, 1964.

Lloyd, Genevieve. *The Man of Reason*. Minneapolis: University of Minnesota Press, 1984.

Lovejoy, Arthur. *The Great Chain of Being*. Cambridge: Harvard University Press, 1936.

Macrae, Robert. " 'Idea' as a Philosophical Term in the Seventeenth Century." *Journal of the History of Ideas* 26 (1965): 175–90.

_____. "Innate Ideas." In *Cartesian Studies*. pp. 32–54. Edited by R. J. Butler. New York: Barnes & Noble, 1972.

McLuhan, Marshall. *The Gutenberg Galaxy*. Toronto: University of Toronto Press, 1962.

Mahler, Margaret. "On the First Three Subphases of the Separation-Individuation Process." *International Journal of Psychoanalysis* 53 (1972): 333–38.

Malcolm, Norman. "Dreaming and Skepticism." In *Meta-Meditations*, pp. 5–25. Edited by Alexander Sesonske and Noel Fleming. Belmont, Ca.: Wadsworth, 1965.

Marcuse, Herbert. *Counter-Revolution and Revolt*. Boston: Beacon, 1972.

Marlies, Mike. "Doubt, Reason and Cartesian Therapy." In *Descartes: Critical and Interpretive Studies*, pp. 89–113. Edited by Michael Hooker. Baltimore: Johns Hopkins Press, 1978.

Marks, Elaine and Courtivron, Isabelle. *New French Feminisms*. New York: Schocken, 1981.

Merchant, Carolyn. *The Death of Nature*. San Francisco: Harper and Row, 1980.

Merleau-Ponty, Maurice. *The Prose of the World*. Translated by John O'Neill. Evanston: Northwestern University Press, 1973.

Montaigne, Michel de. *Essays*. Translated and edited by Donald Frame. New York: St. Martin's Press, 1963.

———. "The Old World and the New." In *The Renaissance Reader*. James Bruce Ross and Mary McLaughlin, eds. Middlesex: Penguin, 1953.

Moussa, Mario. "Infinite Space, Perspective Space." Unpublished paper.

Nagel, Thomas. *The View From Nowhere*. Oxford: Oxford University Press, 1986.

Neville, Robert. *Reconstruction of Thinking*. Albany: State University of New York Press, 1981.

Nietzsche, Frederich. *On the Geneology of Morals*. New York: Vintage, 1969.

———. *The Birth of Tragedy*. New York: Random House, 1967.

Ortega y Gasset, Jose. *Man and Crisis*. New York: Norton, 1958.

Ortner, Sherry. "Is Female to Male as Nature is to Culture?" in *Woman, Culture and Society*, pp. 67–88. Edited by Michele Rosaldo and Louise Lamphere. Stanford: Stanford University Press, 1974.

Panofsky, E. *Renaissance and Renascences in Western Art*. Stockholm: Almquist & Wiksell, 1960.

Pascal, Blaise. *Pensées*. Translated by A. J. Krailsheimer. Hammondsworth, Middlesex: Penguin, 1966.

Piaget, Jean. *Biology and Knowledge*. Chicago: University of Chicago Press, 1971.

———. *Genetic Epistemology*. New York: Columbia University Press, 1970.

———. *Insights and Illusions of Philosophy*. New York: World Publishing, 1965.

———. *Six Psychological Studies*. New York: Random House, 1968a.

———. *Structuralism*. New York: Basic Books, 1970. Originally published in 1968.

_____. *The Child and Reality.* New York: Viking, 1972.

_____. *The Child's Conception of Space.* New York: Norton, 1967.

_____. *The Construction of Reality in the Child.* New York: Random House, 1954.

Piaget, Jean, and Inhelder, Barbel. *The Psychology of the Child.* New York: Harper and Row, 1969.

Plato. *Theatetus and Sophist.* Translated by Francis Cornford. New York: Library of Liberal Arts, 1957.

_____. *Timeaus.* Translated by Benjamin Jowett. Indianapolis: Bobbs-Merrill, 1949.

_____. *Phaedo. The Dialogues of Plato.* Translated by Benjamin Jowett. 4th Edition, rev. Oxford: The Clarendon Press, 1953.

Popkin, Richard. *History of Scepticism from Erasmus to Spinoza.* Berkeley: University of California Press, 1979.

Power, Eileen. "The Position of Women." In *The Legacy of the Middle Ages,* pp. 403–33. Edited by C. G. Crump and E. F. Jacob. New York: Oxford, 1926.

Prichard, H. A. "Descartes' Meditations." In *Descartes: A Collection of Critical Essays,* pp. 140–68. Edited by Willis Doney. Garden City: Doubleday, 1967.

Quine, W. V. O. *Word and Object.* Cambridge: The Technology Press, 1960.

Randall, John Herman. *How Philosophy Uses Its Past.* New York: Columbia University Press, 1963.

Reiss, Timothy. "The Word/World Equation." *Yale French Studies* 49 (1973): 3–12.

Rich, Adrienne. *Of Woman Born.* New York: Bantam, 1976.

Rorty, Richard. *Philosophy and the Mirror of Nature.* Princeton: Princeton University Press, 1979.

Rosaldo, Michele, and Louise Lamphere, eds. *Woman, Culture and Society.* Stanford: Stanford University Press, 1974.

Ross, James, and Mary McLaughlin, eds. *The Renaissance Reader.* New York: Penguin, 1953.

Ross, John. "Towards Fatherhood: The Epigenesis of Paternal Identity During a Boy's First Decade." *International Review of Psychoanalysis,* 4, 1977, pp. 327–47.

Sanday, Peggy Reeve. *Female Power and Male Dominance: On the Origins of Sexual Inequality.* Cambridge: Cambridge University Press, 1981.

Sartre, Jean-Paul. *Being and Nothingness.* New York: Washington Square Press, 1966.

Scharfstein, B.A. "Descartes' Dreams." *The Philosophical Forum,* 1969, p. 323.

Sennett, Richard. *The Uses of Disorder.* New York: Alfred A. Knopf, 1970.

Shakespeare, William. *Hamlet*. New York: Appleton-Century Crofts, 1946.

Stern, Karl. *The Flight From Woman*. New York: Noonday, 1965.

Stout, A. K. "The Basis of Knowledge in Descartes." In *Descartes: A Collection of Critical Essays*, pp. 169–91. Edited by Willis Doney. Garden City: Doubleday, 1967.

Tlumak, Jeffrey. "Certainty and Cartesian Method." In *Descartes: Critical and Interpretive Studies*, pp. 40–73. Edited by Michael Hooker. Baltimore: Johns Hopkins Press, 1978.

Tweyman, Stanley. "The Reliability of Reason." In *Cartesian Studies*, pp. 123–36. Edited by R. J. Butler. New York: Barnes & Noble, 1972.

Vicinus, Martha. *Suffer and Be Still*. Bloomington: Indiana University Press, 1972.

Walsh, W. H. *Metaphysics*. London: Hutchinson University Library, 1963.

Weiss, Roberto. "Scholarship from Petrarch to Erasmus." In *The Age of the Renaissance*, pp. 119–44. Edited by Denis Hay. New York: McGraw-Hill, 1967.

Whitehead, Alfred North. *Adventures of Ideas*. 1933; reprint ed., New York: Collier Macmillan, 1967.

_____. *Science and the Modern World*. 1925; reprint ed., Toronto: Collier Macmillan, 1967.

Williams, Bernard. *Descartes: the Project of Pure Inquiry*. Hammondsworth, Middlesex: Penguin, 1978.

Wilshire, Bruce. *The Eclipse of University Teaching: Dynamics of Purification and Exclusion*. Manuscript in progress.

Wilson, Margaret. "Cartesian Dualism." In *Descartes: Critical and Interpretive Studies*, pp. 197–211. Edited by Michael Hooker. Baltimore: Johns Hopkins Press, 1978.

_____. *Descartes*. London: Routledge and Kegan Paul, 1978.

Wisdon, J. "Three Dreams of Descartes" *International Journal of Psychoanalysis*, 28, pp. 118–28.

Wittgenstein, Ludwig. *The Blue and Brown Books*. Oxford: Basil Blackwell, 1969.

Index

Absolutism: and social disorder, 17;
Cartesian, 17, 22, 29, 58
Alberti, Leon Batista, 54, 64, 67, 68
Alexander, Robert, 28, 43
Anxiety: and separation from the mother,
57–58, 106–107; cultural, and female
generativity, 109–112; cultural, and
separation from maternal cosmos, 5, 58,
59, 100, 112; cultural, Cartesian reaction-
formations to, 100, 106, 108; in
Descartes's dreams, 1; in *Meditations*, 4, 5,
10, 13, 43, 51, 57, 60, 61, 100, 108
Apple-basket simile, 16–17, 39, 43
Aries, Philippe, 70, 127
Aristotle, 35, 50, 52, 68, 93, 104
Art, medieval, 60–66, 122–123: absence of
perspective in, 60, 63–66; representation
of space in, 62–64
Art, perspective in. *See* Perspective: in art
Ashworth, E. J., 92
Augustine, 55, 79, 80, 81, 93

Bacon, Francis, 8, 75, 100, 104, 105, 109,
112, 125–127
Barfield, Owen, 8, 48, 53, 55, 59, 60, 69,
71, 72, 73, 103
Baxandall, Michael, 54, 64, 67, 122, 123,
124
Bergson, Henri, 103
Berkeley, 27
Berman, Morris, 2, 4, 8, 48, 53, 73, 103,
116
Bernstein, Richard, 4
Beyond the Pleasure Principle, 105
Birth: as image of emergence of modernity,
5, 58, 59, 97–8, 100. *See also* "Drama of
parturition"; medical practices, changes
in the seventeenth century, 109, 128;
rebirth as Cartesian theme, 97, 100, 105,
106, 108

Body, The. *See also* Dualism, Mind-Body:
childhood and, 56, 76, 91, 97; as
impediment to knowledge, for Descartes,
26, 56, 89–90, 94–95, 97–98; as machine,
94; Greek view of, 94; medieval
philosophy and, 9, 45; philosophers'
disdain for, 76, 93; transcendence of, in
Meditations, 76, 88, 90–92, 94; women's
body as object of anxiety and rage, 110,
111
Brown, Norman O., 107
Brunelleschi, 63, 67, 68
Bruno, Giordano, 68
Burtt, E. A., 34, 35, 69

Capra, Fritjof, 2, 116
Caton, Hiram, 80, 125
Chamberlin, E. R., 41
Childhood: 47, 130; and the body, 56, 91,
97, 98; cultural views of, seventeenth-
century, 126–7; Descartes' view of, 97–98,
108; "discovery" of, 130
Chodorow, Nancy, 6, 112, 113, 115, 130
Cogito, The, 25–26, 86
Cognitive Development: correspondence
with Cartesian themes, 30–31;
correspondence with cultural
development, 8, 10, 29, 45–49, 55–57;
Descartes on, 56, 57; egocentrism and,
46, 56, 121–122; gender differences and,
6–7, 113; inner/outer distinction and,
55–56; objectivity and, 30, 46; perception
of space and, 61–62; "permanent object
concept" and, 30; Piaget on, 30, 46, 47,
55; self/world distinction and, 29, 46, 55
Cohen, Avner, 4, 122
Consciousness: Cartesian notion of, 50;
medieval notion of, 53; "participating
consciousness," 48, 53, 100, 103. *See also*
Inwardness; Mind

141

Copernicus, 34, 46, 68
Cultural Relativism, 40–43, 45; "cultural
    norm," notion of, 42; Descartes on, 42;
    Montaigne on, 40–41

Da Vinci, Leonardo, 54
Danto, Arthur, 76
deBeauvoir, Simone, 107
Developmental Theory, 4, 6, 7, 57, 106
Dewey, John, 4, 17, 51, 76, 77, 87, 116
Discontinuity of human experience, 28, 30.
    See also Mind, Descartes's image of
Dinnerstein, Dorothy, 7, 11, 129
Doney, Willis, 15, 126
Donne, John, 14, 59
Doubt, Cartesian, 10, 14–18, 20–21, 28, 73,
    80; as authentic, 6; as experiential, 17; as
    methodical, 15–16; "by inattention," 28,
    31; contemporary analytic philosophy
    and, 14–15; instability of, 22, 31;
    mystification and, 18, 20–21; pervasive
    nature of, 14; Pyrhonnian scepticism
    and, 14
Douglas, Mary, 17, 77, 81, 124
"Drama of Parturition," 5, 6, 11, 59, 62, 70,
    100, 110–112
Dream Argument in *Meditations*, 18–21
Dreams, Descartes's, 1, 14, 100
Dualism, Mind-Body, 26; Cartesian, 93–94;
    in Western philosophical tradition, 93
Durer, Albrecht, 64

Easlea, Brian, 4, 108, 109, 110, 128, 129
Edgerton, Samuel Jr., 63, 65, 66, 123
Egocentrism. *See* Cognitive Development
Ehrenreich, Barbara, 108, 128
Elizabeth of Bohemia, 14, 90
Emotions, 76; Descartes on, 85, 89, 126
Empiricism, 3, 105, 111
English, Dierdre, 108
"Epistemological Fallenness," 43, 79
Error: Descartes notion of, 37–38, 50, 51,
    78–81; medieval notion of, 51
Evans, J. L., 80
Evil. *See* "Problem of evil"
Evil Genius, 18, 20, 21, 23–24, 27, 43
External World. *See* Self/World distinction

Febvre, Lucien, 69, 70
Female Cosmos. *See* Nature as Female

"Feminine, The"; epistemological values
    and, 9, 100, 102–103, 112, 114;
    seventeenth-century "flight from the
    feminine," 5, 9, 100, 108–112;
    transcendence of, 9. *See also* Woman, fear
    of
Feminism: contemporary sociological
    emphasis, 112, 113–114; French and
    American, comparison, 131; in
    Nineteenth-century, 114; re-visioning of
    knowledge, 103, 112, 114, 115, 131;
    political movement, 115
Feyerabend, Paul, 77
"Flight from the Feminine," *See* Feminine,
    The
Foucault, Michel, 3, 5, 117
Frankfurt, Harry, 15, 105
Freedom, Cartesian doctrine of, 84–85
Freud, Sigmund, 105, 107, 127
Furth, Hans, 47

Galileo, Galilei, 34, 36–37, 45, 50
Gassendi, 88, 92
Gender: cognitive development and, 6–7,
    105, 112–113, 130; differences, as social
    construction, 113–114; scientific
    metaphors and, 104, 105, 112
Gewirth, Alan, 92, 126
Gibson, James, 64, 65, 122
Gilligan, Carol, 6, 7, 103, 112, 115, 130, 131
Gillispie, Charles, 99, 102
Gilmore, Myron, 69, 70
Gilson, Etienne, 80
God: as infinite, 124; as epistemological
    metaphor, 81; as paternal image, 58, 108,
    110; Augustinian "problem of evil" and,
    78–81; Cartesian problem of error and,
    78–81; Descartes's concept of, 27, 81;
    Descartes's philosophical need of, 21–22,
    28, 38, 61, 86
Greene, Marjorie, 35, 73
Guillen, Claudio, 54, 123
Gynocentric cultures, 129, 130

Hacking, Ian, 130
Hale, J. R., 41, 42
Hamlyn, D. W., 47
Harding, Sandra, 3, 104, 115, 127, 131
Harries, Karsten, 4, 43, 68, 121, 123
Harth, Erica, 127